H. W. Smith

Hiram Orcutt.

THE

PARENTS' MANUAL;

OR,

HOME AND SCHOOL TRAINING.

BY

HIRAM ORCUTT, A.M.,

Author of "The Class-Book of Prose and Poetry," "Gleanings from School-Life Experience," and "The Teacher's Manual."

"To teach, whether by word or action, is the greatest function on earth." CHANNING.

BOSTON:

PUBLISHED BY THOMPSON, BROWN, & CO.,

25 AND 29, CORNHILL.

1874

Boston:
Rand Avery, & Co., Stereotypers and Printers.

TO

THE FAITHFUL MOTHERS IN AMERICA,

WHO REGARD THEIR HOMES AS THEIR KINGDOM, AND THE POLISHING OF THEIR "JEWELS" AS THEIR PRIDE AND CHIEF GLORY,

THIS VOLUME,

WHICH HAS BEEN WRITTEN FOR THE AID AND ENCOURAGEMENT OF ALL WHO SUSTAIN PARENTAL RELATIONS,

IS RESPECTFULLY DEDICATED BY

THE AUTHOR.

PREFACE.

The family and the school are inseparably connected in the great work of education; yet much the larger share of the labor and responsibility necessarily belongs to parents. Teachers are only their assistants and employés, having delegated authority and power; and their success and usefulness depend largely upon the wisdom and co-operation of their employers. Hence the discipline of the family embraces the discipline of the school, and should be based upon the same principles, and studied with equal care and earnestness both by parents and teachers.

With these views, and with the hope of aiding in the noble work of training our American children for greater usefulness and a higher destiny than we have yet realized, the author has prepared this volume. "The Parents' Manual" is designed as the counterpart of "THE TEACHER'S MANUAL," published two years ago. That volume treated upon the teacher's duties to his pupils in all the relations he sustains to the school: this treats upon parents' duties in all the relations they sustain to their children, in the family, in the school, and in society, during the period of their minority.

The author is not aware that any one book covering the same ground has ever been written upon this subject. His aim has been to make the work concise and practical. How far and how well he has accomplished his object, he must leave to the reader to judge.

TILDEN SEMINARY,
WEST LEBANON, N.H., April, 1874.

CONTENTS.

THE PARENTS' MANUAL.

I.

INTRODUCTION.

"Home is the sacred refuge of our life."
DRYDEN.

THE home of childhood, — what hallowed associations cluster around it! How sacred to the memory and dear to the heart that has felt its power! The place is consecrated by parental and filial affection, and by innocent sports and joys, which can never be repeated in the experience of life. The very *name* excites emotions which no language can describe. And when the melody of

"Home, home, sweet, sweet home!"

strikes upon the ear, the fountains of the soul are stirred to their lowest depths.

Here exist the most intimate and endearing of all human relations. Husband and wife, parents and children, brothers and sisters, constitute the home, and enjoy a common sympathy, and toil together to promote the common good.

The home was first planted in Eden by God's own hand, and has been transplanted into every civilized community. In these family relations the father stands as the ordained head of his household, — to provide for their wants, promote their happiness, and share their blessings. The mother is his "helpmeet," his honored queen, and the sharer of his authority and responsibility in the important work of education: indeed, she is the central light and animating spirit of every true home; and hence from her emanates the educating and moulding power in every family.

The importance of this home to the welfare of our race cannot be overestimated. It is the heart, whose arteries extend to the utmost limits of human society, and from which flows the life-blood of the nation. If this blood is pure, it imparts health and vigor to the whole body politic; but, if impure, it engenders corruption, disease, and death.

Now, if home-training is so important, and the mother is the chief source of that influence which develops and matures all that is noble in the future citizen, it must follow that the legitimate sphere of her activity and usefulness lies chiefly in her own household. If she does well the work which has been assigned her there, she will have no time, nor strength, nor disposition, to seek another and more extensive field of labor.

II.

PARENTAL RESPONSIBILITY.

WHO can measure it? Parents are the God-commissioned guardians, rulers, and guides of their children. They have been selected from the race, and ordained to this special work. Implanted in them is an instinctive, peculiar love for their offspring, which was designed to insure fidelity. United by the ties of consanguinity, they are the nearest in affection, and the nearest in place. In this fearful position, parents have in charge the beginning and shaping of a boundless, eternal destiny. As rulers and teachers, they hold a sceptre more royal than that of kings, and occupy a throne nearest of any human power to the throne of God. Parents are therefore ordained as special ministers, to keep safely, educate wisely, and bless continually, their tender children.

Mark the filial spirit which the child cherishes for the fond and faithful mother. What more pure and elevating? With what simple and unfaltering faith does he lean upon the maternal arm, and trust in maternal fidelity! Every tone of the mother's voice thrills the heart of childhood; and every expression of her countenance awakens joy or sorrow, hope or fear. Here we have a glimpse of the unmeasured power of home-training over the destiny of the child, which is the measure of parental responsibility; yet no finite mind can ever fully comprehend it.

And for what are parents training their children? They enjoy them now as sunbeams which cheer their homes, and hold them as treasures which wealth could not purchase. They hope to have them as companions in riper years, and to lean upon them for comfort and support in declining life. But it will depend largely upon their early training whether they will honor or dishonor the name they have inherited; whether they will be a source of comfort and joy, or will "bring the gray hairs of their parents in sorrow to their graves."

Parents are training their children also for society, for the duties and responsibilities of citizenship. But what kind of citizenship shall it be? "The child is the father of the man;" and his development for good or evil, under parental control, will determine his future character. The neglect or mismanagement of parents results in the misdeeds of children. The ill-tempered and disobedient boy, unsubdued at home, will be disorderly at school, and contentious, vulgar, and profane in the streets; and he is thus trained to enter directly upon a course of dissipation and crime that may lead to ruin. The unrestrained girl will be likely to grow up self-willed, petulant, vain, frivolous, and self-idolizing; and society made up of such citizens will become a mingled scene of struggling and crushing antagonisms. Let it not be forgotten that the thirty thousand human beings now confined within prison-walls in the United States were once innocent children in maternal arms. What a fearful responsibility, then, rests upon American parents, since the destiny of their children and of the nation depends upon their influence and efforts!

Again: the family is a school, and the parents the divinely-ordained teachers. Education begins at the dawn of existence, and terminates only with life. Helpless infancy is intrusted to parental love and care. Its puny body must be nourished and clothed. With what provident care has the Creator provided for these special wants! and how tenderly does the true mother watch over her precious charge, and minister to its necessities and comforts! Anxious days and sleepless nights bear testimony to her faithfulness. Ere long, through the development of the physical system, intelligence dawns; and smiles begin to play upon the countenance, as if the child had learned to recognize with gratitude and love the patient toil of its benefactor. During this period its very life was in peril, dependent upon the mother, the guardian angel of the home.

Here opens another scene in life's drama. With intelligence come the activity and accountability of the child, and a new responsibility upon the parent. The tiny limbs must be trained to walk, and the silent tongue to prattle. The mind, like a clean white canvas, begins now to receive impressions from the external world through the senses, and to judge of the right and wrong of childish actions. Here double diligence must be exercised to guard against new danger, — not the danger of being harmed by fire or water or poison through ignorance of their uses and abuses, but by the corrupting influence of a wicked world. And how can parents feel less solicitude for the moral safety of their children who have come to years of discretion, and are compelled to walk amid so many pitfalls of ruin, than for their physical safety while exposed to the common accidents of life?

At this critical period, provision must be made to form the character; to expand, mature, and furnish the mind; to cultivate the conscience; in a word, to develop the whole being into true manhood or womanhood. This is the end to be reached, and by a process which is expressed by the word "education;" and this vast work is intrusted chiefly to parents. For its accomplishment they are held responsible; and this responsibility they cannot evade.

III.

PARENTAL CONTROL.

THE discipline of the family, as treated in this volume, implies much more than family government: it includes the management and culture of children in all the relations they sustain while under parental care. But parental control and filial submission are not only a duty under the divine law, but a necessity for the welfare of the child. Without experience, he is in the midst of danger, and exposed to injury and death; and yet he fears no evil. His hand must be forcibly withheld from the burning coals; and, though he cry ever so bitterly, he must not be allowed to play with edged tools, nor to eat poison. The most strenuous advocates of moral suasion must admit that here, at least, authority and force are properly and necessarily exercised. And it is just here that the child is initiated into submission to the power above him. In every instance of positive and immediate danger, the parent interferes to prevent the evil; and yet how many utterly fail to administer positive government beyond this point! Such neglect is entirely inconsistent and ruinous. Government, to be effective, must be absolute and uniform, and must reach every case of *wrong* as well as of danger.

The child has been described by some writer as "a little crawling, creeping, picking, pulling, pushing, climbing, tottling, and tumbling piece of activity." As such he is committed to the mother's care. Activity is, indeed, a condition of his mental and physical development;

but it must be under constant control. With a blind impulse he moves in every direction, regardless alike of his own safety and of the comforts and rights of others. He may pull the boiling teapot from the stove; and may not the mother force him away to prevent his death from scalding? He may dash the china set upon the floor; and may she not, with equal propriety, interpose her authority to prevent the destruction of the property, and to teach the child the wrong of such recklessness? Suppose she meets angry wilfulness and sullen resistance in her efforts to correct and restrain: may she not, and should she not, hold the little rebel under discipline until he is subdued to cheerful obedience?

There must be fixed statutes in every domestic realm; and these must be revealed to the children as soon as they can understand them, and must be repeated as often as they are disposed to violate them. And these laws must be enforced at all times and everywhere if the desirable results of family government are to be realized. The habit of disobedience, which often results from parental weakness, may lead to some terrible, blighting calamity to the family. How often are we startled by news of the sudden and violent death of some darling child! But, had that child been taught unconditional obedience to parental authority, he would not have entered the forbidden water, nor played upon the brink of the precipice. Begin early to enforce obedience, and with a steady hand, firm purpose, and loving heart, meet and subdue every rebellious effort on the part of the child, and family government will be comparatively easy, and the fearful consequences of insubordination will be avoided. Immediate submission to separate and incidental commands and prohibitions is the only condition of absolute parental control and filial security. This should be insisted on from the beginning. I do not believe in the "divine right of kings;" but I do insist upon the divine right of parents to *control* their children during all the years of their minority; and that the future character of these children, as pupils, as citizens, and as subjects of the divine government, will be determined largely by this early training.

It is from the ranks of children ungoverned at home that our reform-schools, houses of correction, jails, and prisons are filled; and the domestic training that saves from such fearful consequences begins by securing obedience to specific directions, and expands into a cheerful compliance with general rules of right and duty. If the child is not required to obey a particular command, he will not conform to general laws in the family, in the school, or in society: but if, on the other hand, filial obedience *early* becomes a habit, the severer struggles between parents and children which cause so much pain and grief in after-years would be avoided; and that "stubborn will" which defies parental authority, and invokes severe punishments, would never be formed.

This was evidently a part of the divine plan. At first, the child is not only ignorant and impulsive, but weak, and easily controlled. Soon consciousness dawns, and he begins to recognize the mother's voice and smile. Fear, love, and reverence are awakened; and these become powerful aids to maternal government. This, then, is the opportunity, and these the means provided by God, to enforce the great lesson, and to teach the child not only the necessity, but the obligation, of obedience.

Happy are those children who have been thus reared under the discipline of home; happy in the peaceful submission to parental authority, and in the enjoyment of parental love; happy in the exercise of filial affection, and reverence toward those whom God has placed over them; and happy in the enjoyment of mutual love and mutual sympathy. And happy, indeed, those parents whose fidelity has trained for themselves, their country, and their God, *such* a family; happy in their society and in the sunshine of their affections; happy in the thought that they will be sustained and comforted in declining life by the strong arm and tender heart of their own loyal offspring, and that they will die, not among strangers, but surrounded by their own kindred; happy in the assurance that their children will in the future honor their name, their memory, and their virtues, and will bless the nation through the influence of a noble and exalted citizenship.

IV.

PARENTAL MISMANAGEMENT.

FAMILY government is both an art and a science. Some parents are endowed by nature with a special gift to manage and control children; while others seem almost entirely to lack this qualification. The first class, even, may profit by suggestions from the more experienced and wise; but the second class, who must also bear parental responsibility, especially need instruction and training for their important work.

Insubordination is a characteristic of our age and country. It is seen in the irreverent and unruly spirit of children in the family and in the school; in their rude, boisterous, and profane conduct in the streets; in their truancy and crime, which have filled our reform-schools and houses of correction; in the frequent rebellions in academies and colleges throughout the land. That all these consequences have too often resulted directly from parental inefficiency and mismanagement, no intelligent observer can doubt.

Some parents, through their own perverseness, have lost the power to minister at the sacred family altar. Their example and influence are wholly unfavorable to wholesome discipline. They sustain the sacred relation of husband and wife, and have been intrusted with the holy mission of moulding the character of childhood; but they have become divorced in spirit and in life. Their little differences are permitted to ripen into open rupture; and their home, which should be the very paradise of earthly bliss, where affection and harmony always dwell, becomes a scene of perpetual strife and turmoil. And how fearful the influence of such example over the immediate and more distant future of these children! A large proportion of the lawlessness, vice, and crime, which curse American society, results directly from this cause. Here, then, is a theme for the contemplation of the Christian philanthropist, who seeks the elevation of our people and the perpetuity of our free institutions. Let him toil to harmonize, purify, and enlighten the *homes* where our future citizens must be trained.

Other parents do not attempt to govern their children, nor believe in the importance or utility of such control, except in cases of absolute physical danger: hence they offer no restraints, and exercise no authority over them. They profess to believe that reproofs and punishments result only in moroseness of disposition, and perverseness of manners. Such interpositions disturb the quiet and harmony of the family; and hence the parents yield to every wish, and gratify every desire, of their children, to avoid the fancied evil. But *such* a family democracy soon resolves itself into a fearful despotism, where the *children* are the rulers, and their parents are the obedient and much-abused subjects. How wise (in their own estimation), arrogant, dictatorial, and ill-mannered such children become, we have frequent opportunities to see. Nor could it be otherwise, under this perverted order of things. The divinely-appointed sovereigns of the house have been deposed, and are in subjection. The natural subjects have never learned obedience under authority: hence the sad consequences are realized at home, in school, and in society.

Still other parents attempt to govern, but fail, some from one cause, and some from another. I may here specify some of the more common ways of *spoiling* children.

First, I will name the *fickle* method. Parental tenderness was designed by God to insure fidelity. It inspires an undying interest in the child's welfare; and, if rightly directed, will secure its object. But the mother lacks firmness. Her convictions are all right, and her views of government, in the main, correct; but she seems to have no power to resist her child's importunity. He craves some improper gratification, and demands indulgence. The mother refuses. The child persists, because he has learned by experience that she does not really mean *no* when she says it. Why did she not teach her darling that important lesson in the beginning, and thus save herself all this trouble and annoyance? She did not; and hence the child undertakes to reverse her decision, and with the full assurance that he can accomplish his object. It may cost a half-hour's teasing, or a "flood of tears," or a violent fit of passion, or a spasmodic display of affection, as the case may be; but the worn and weary mother will surely yield. The contest is only a matter of time: the result is not doubtful. And what is the influence of this fickleness upon the temper and life of the child? Does he love his mother more tenderly? Is he more amiable, gentle, obedient, and faithful afterwards? No: he will become more irritable and selfish, more demanding and determined in his efforts to secure his object. Develop the selfish propensities of a child's nature, and his filial love will be diminished in the same proportion. The former is allowed to overgrow and cover up the latter. That mother is the most earnestly loved by her children who governs them with a firm and impartial hand, whose decision always settles all questions without controversy, and whose promises are sure of fulfilment. Let parents carefully consider the requests of their children asking indulgence; and, when they have said *yes* or *no*, let that always be understood to be the *final* decision.

Second, Another method of spoiling children I will call the *impulsive.* Parents practising this method of government are *fitful.* They act towards their children as they feel at the time. In their genial mood, unbounded indulgence is allowed them: they discover no faults to be corrected; and will allow no punishments to be inflicted, either at home or at school. And yet, when the fit of passion comes on, they assail their children with violence, and chastise them in an unmerciful manner, and by means wholly unjustifiable under any judicious system of training. Pinching, pushing, cuffing, flogging, thumping, and shutting up in the dark closet, are among the penalties inflicted. These unfortunate children soon learn to enjoy the sunshine, and to endure the storm; but the influence of such treatment upon their temper, habits, and life, is fearful. They have no confidence in the management of their parents, and can cherish for them but a limited amount of affection. They grow up ill-tempered, fretful, and disobedient, wholly unfitted for the duties and responsibilities of mature life.

Third, I will allude to the *scolding* and *threatening* methods of spoiling children. Correction and reproof are proper and necessary in family government; but constant fault-finding is wrong and ruinous. To ignore the good, and always censure the bad, tends to discourage the child, and leaves him to contract habits of heedlessness, and to float along the current of passion and evil influence, regardless of consequences. His good qualities and commendable conduct should be recognized, and encouraged by kind words of approval. In this way, that pride of character and self-respect may be cultivated which will prevent much of the wrong that parents are obliged to rebuke and punish.

The habit of threatening children is equally objectionable. The desire of the parent is to enforce obedience without severity; but the result is very different. Obedience is not rendered, and the failure to secure it by threatening disarms authority. Not only so, but every unexecuted threat gives the child an example of falsehood. What does he care about the oft-repeated assurance that he will be "shut up in the dark closet," or "sent to the cellar," or "skinned alive," since he knows that neither the imprisonment nor the skinning is likely to follow? Or if, by chance, the threatened punishment is undertaken, the child well understands his own ability to win in the fight. He has learned to control such parental weakness, and gain his object; and he will not fail to improve every opportunity. And, when the actions of parents so often contradict their words, children will naturally learn the lesson, and contract the habit of lying. What a harvest of insubordination and misery has been reaped in those families which have been reared under such mismanagement!

To avoid the contemplated evil, let parents adopt the following negative rules: —

Never threaten unless you design to execute.

Never threaten a specific punishment for an anticipated offence.

Never resort to stratagem in the management of children.

These are indeed *golden rules* in family discipline; and, if strictly followed, will "hide a multitude of sins."

Fourth, The *flogging* method of spoiling children must not be overlooked.

I do not mean to call in question the propriety and necessity of sometimes resorting to severity in the government of children. There are times when, literally, to "spare the rod" is to "spoil the child." There are cases in the treatment of which the severest punishment is not only the first and only remedy, but an expression of the greatest kindness; and this severity is more often made necessary by the mismanagement of parents than by any other cause.

The system of family government

which I here condemn adopts "flogging" as a rule. It offers a blow for every offence. It does not recognize kindness as the necessary acompaniment of severity, and management as a better way of preventing evil. Corporal punishment so employed appeals to the lower nature of the child, and hence does not secure the object.

I once called to account, for a slight offence, a little boy seven years of age who had been intrusted to my care. I said to him, "Now, Bertie, what shall I do with you for thus disobeying my orders?" His answer was, "Whip me, of course." The little fellow had been so roughly treated in his home relations, that he knew of no other disciplinary agency but "flogging;" and expected this for every act of disobedience. And he supposed still further, that this penalty, like penance, atoned for the crime.

Hence he must infer that the fear of punishment is the only motive to obedience. View this system as we may, it tends to subvert the true idea of discipline, and to degrade its subjects in the scale of moral beings. No well-managed and well-governed family needs such treatment; and no wise and judicious parent ever resorts to it.

Fifth, The *persuasive* is still another method of spoiling children.

Persuasion, and every other mild measure which tends to induce good behavior, are legitimate agencies in family government. The moral power of gentleness, forbearance, kindness, good example, wholesome counsel, and proffered reward, should be recognized, as well as the moral power of reproof and punishment; but none of these may ever take the place of authority.

But the liability of mistake is not in

the use, but in the *abuse*, of gentle measures in the training of the young. Moral suasion has its own proper sphere, in the management of the family, to prevent evil. When the passions are unruffled, and the loyalty of our children is unquestioned, it is Godlike to win and control them by the power of affection. It is proper, also, to rebuke and chastise when they have abused our love, and broken away from our authority. This spirit of disobedience manifests itself in different ways, according to the disposition of the child and the circumstances of the case, — sometimes in cool and deliberate disregard of our wishes, sometimes in sullen and determined hostility, sometimes in passion that vents itself in screams and angry tears, and sometimes in open resistance. In either case, it is wrong and ruinous to attempt to *coax* him into obedience. The effort may succeed, and it may fail: it makes but little difference which. Authority, which is the only legitimate controlling power in such cases, has either been entirely set aside, or greatly weakened by an appeal to argument. To resort to persuasion, therefore, is a confession of weakness, and a loss of governing power.

Sixth, Nearly allied to the persuasive is the *bribing* method of spoiling children.

Here, again, let me not be misunderstood. I do not condemn the principle of rewarding fidelity in family government. This is just and proper when rightly applied. But rewarding spontaneous and voluntary obedience on the part of the child is quite another thing from offering rewards to *induce* or *restore* good behavior. In the first case, real merit is compensated; in the second, a price is paid the child for doing what obligation and duty demand of all. In the former instance, there is an acknowledged allegiance to parental control, and submission to parental authority; in the latter, the proffered reward becomes the prevailing motive to action, and loyalty is sacrificed to selfishness. Paying children for being good is not the exercise of authority, nor can it secure obedience. It is a ruinous bargain, — a bounty upon impudence and insubordination. In all such traffic, disobedience becomes a currency in the family market to purchase any desired indulgence. If a slight offence will induce the mother to give a single piece of pie, cake, or candy, to her rebellious child, stubbornness will purchase more, and a fierce open war still more, to gratify a craving, perverted palate, and to weaken the sense of filial obligation. The price paid for a tardy compliance with parental commands induces the child to act from wrong motives, and hence becomes a bribe in the hands of the parent. Who can fail to see the fearful train of evils that must follow such a process of family government? And yet is not a better method than those here described, when adopted, the exception, and not the rule, in our American families?

V.

PARENTAL EFFICIENCY.

I MAY now inquire for the true method of family government. It is based upon divinely-established authority. The very relations of parents and children demand absolute and unconditional control on the one hand, and obedience on the other.

But this obedience is not, like filial love and faith, *instinctive.* Every child of common capacity turns to his mother for food, and, with instinctive confidence, seeks her sympathy and protection in the hour of fright and danger. He cannot be *taught* to love and confide in that mother; for affection and confidence spring up *spontaneously* in the young heart. But not so with obedience. The mother sometimes wonders and is grieved that her darling, so affectionate, so confiding, and so dependent, does not always and instantly regard her wishes and obey her commands. But I can tell her the reason. That child has no natural impulse in that direction; has no idea of submission. The habit of obedience is yet to be created under parental discipline, and is wholly the work of education. Hence it must follow that insubordination in the family is not so much the fault of children as of their parents. Had the mother, fully conscious of her right and duty in this regard, employed her authority and strength to secure obedience to her commands during infancy and childhood, stubbornness would be unknown in that family. Should she, then, become angry with her children for faults which her own neglect has cultivated and encouraged? The child must be *taught* obedience. The mother has failed to enforce that lesson, and hence her disappointment and grief. In the exercise of mistaken kindness, she failed to check the first indications of insubordination, and thus lost control over her child, and laid the foundation for the misrule and ruin which naturally follow. But it may not be too late, even now, for her to establish her authority, and correct the evil. Let her do this without delay, and by any proper means necessary.

And how shall this authority be exercised so as to prevent the consequences of disobedience? Authority, like gravity in the material world, must always be the controlling power in the family; but it may generally be concealed. It is "a power behind the throne," always acknowledged and constant in its influence;

but its sceptre is invisible. It operates without friction, and holds in subjection the conflicting and struggling passions during the forming periods of childhood and youth.

Authority is mild and gentle in its more effective aspects. When the mother makes it the basis of her government, it is not necessary for her to assume sternness and severity towards her children, nor to command them in a harsh and abrupt manner. The more gentle, courteous, and kind in her expressions, the better, if they understand them as the mandates of authority, to be instantly obeyed. Even the reasons for her requirements may be explained, when she can properly leave the child to reflect upon the course of conduct recommended, with a view of securing his approval. But, if a question of obedience is pending, no reasons should be given.

The principle of simple submission to authority must first be settled, and cheerful compliance secured. Reasons should never be offered as inducements to secure obedience. If the mother stops to parley with her rebellious child, he will surely gain the victory.

Nor is this view of our subject inconsistent with indulgence. The mother may indulge her children in all that is beneficial and harmless, and forbear with them when in fault, and yet exercise over them absolute and supreme control. Indeed, this very indulgence increases her power to control them; and, when her authority is justly and gently exercised, it serves to strengthen their love and confidence. But, when maternal authority is sacrificed in an attempt to win and hold childish affection, it is always a failure. Children enjoy, for the time, the mother's *excessive* indulgence;

but they soon learn her weakness. As years roll on, insubordination becomes intolerable, and severe punishments necessary. Then they come to view her imbecility with mingled emotions of pity and contempt. Indulgence, without government, always tends to this result; and just here the mistake is made in family discipline. The only way to gain the lasting love and gratitude of our children is to *govern* them. Nor is there, as I have already intimated, any antagonism between free indulgence and absolute control. Of course, they must be restrained in every thing that is dangerous or injurious; but they may be gratified to any extent, and safely, in every thing that is harmless, so long as they cheerfully yield to acknowledged authority.

Another principle of great importance underlies family discipline. The child must never gain any desired object by disobedience; must never be gratified by doing wrong. The favors bestowed must reward only fidelity and submission. And, still further, inconvenience, privation, or pain, must attend and follow every act of transgression. This is according to the divine plan, after which family government should be modelled.

And it must be *certain* that merited punishment will follow *every* wrong act. To illustrate: The child approaches too near the fire, or puts his fingers into the blaze of the candle; and, every time, he suffers pain as a consequence. The result is, he soon learns obedience to Nature's law, and keeps at a proper distance from the fire. A *slight* pain, and the positive certainty of suffering, have accomplished the object. Now for the application: Let the mother see to it that *every time* her child disobeys her commands, or disregards her wishes, he will suffer for the wrong, and she will seldom have occasion to inflict *severe* penalties. The *certainty* more than the *severity* of the punishment makes it effectual. I will call this treatment *mild severity*, and commend it to every thoughtful parent. If attended by steadiness, firmness, and decision, it will accomplish much more than scolding, threatening, and whipping.

Another important thought in this connection. As far as possible, let the punishment be the natural consequence of the fault which has been committed. For instance: Suppose the child always throws down his hat which he is required to hang upon the rack, and the mother wishes to correct the habit. She may require him to return and hang up his hat, and, as a penalty for the first offence, detain him five minutes before he is allowed to return to his play; for the second offence, ten minutes; and so on until the habit is cured. Here the privation is associated with the fault, and seems naturally to result from it. The child has time for reflection, and feels the influence of a strong motive to reform. Or suppose the child is allowed a recess from study, say for thirty minutes, but he remains at play for *forty* minutes. Let the mother punish him by shortening his recess, first to *twenty* minutes, then to *ten*, and finally allow him *no* time for play until she is assured that he will return promptly as directed.

All such punishments are designed to correct and cure the evil for the future benefit of the child. They may be mild or severe as the case requires, but should never be vindictive, nor administered in anger. Promptness and firmness are demanded in correcting the faults of children, but harshness and ill-temper never.

Kindness and sympathy are powerful disciplinary agencies, and should always accompany reproof and severity. Let the child be made to understand that every look of disapprobation, every word of rebuke, and every penalty inflicted, is prompted by maternal love, and the very fact will tend strongly to subdue the rebellious spirit. And mutual sympathy between parents and children operates to secure the same result. Look at the natural effect of sympathy in its material and mental aspects. The habits of one person are imparted to the whole company: cheerfulness and joy, or sorrow and sadness, expressed by one individual, carry either happiness or gloom to the hearts of the circle in which he mingles. It is through sympathy that mankind gain control over each other in the common affairs of life. They cherish the feelings and embrace the opinions of those they love; and, if these opinions are changed in maturer years, it is more the result of sympathy than argument. Hence we can readily understand the power of this principle over childhood. The child is in full sympathy with the true mother, clings to her in the hour of danger, believes and confides in her with unwavering confidence, imitates her actions, treasures up her words, and imbibes her very feelings and emotions. This results partly from the intimate relations they sustain to each other, and partly from judicious training. The degree of love and confidence which the child cherishes for his mother depends upon the amount of sincere sympathy she manifests in his childish hopes and fears, joys and sorrows, recreations and amusements, ideas and fancies. The more childlike the parent, the better qualified she is to manage and guide her household. Hence the great importance of gaining the confidence and love of our children, and the still greater necessity of being ourselves, in character and life, what we desire them to become.

We have no right to expect that these children will *naturally* do right, rather than wrong. Facts are against such a conclusion. Indeed, accountability presupposes instruction as to what is right and wrong; and, when they begin to recognize this distinction, both the good and the bad in their conduct should have our attention. We should not only rebuke and punish the wrong, but also commend the right with equal fidelity. Serious mistakes are often made in dealing with the principle here involved. For illustration: The child tells the truth many times during the week, and, in some instances, under special provocation to deceive; but the mother regards truth-telling as a matter of course, and offers no commendation. Finally the temptation becomes too strong, and the child tells a falsehood, — one lie against many instances of truth-telling; and he is assailed at once with reproaches and punishments. The reproof and chastisement may be proper, both in kind and degree; but, if the mother has failed to commend her child for his fidelity, she has omitted the most important part of her duty. Such encouragement would tend to form and strengthen the habit of well-doing, and to weaken the power of evil. To commend pure thoughts, correct motives, and right actions, is to aid the child in his efforts to establish a character of integrity and uprightness.

I do not mean by these suggestions to encourage the indiscriminate praise and flattery of children by their parents. This would defeat the end in view by cultivating vanity and self-conceit. Praise what is praiseworthy, rebuke what is wrong; and the influence of parental discipline will tend to develop only the more noble elements of character.

There is one instance where the mother *never* makes a mistake in the application of this principle; viz., while her children are learning the arts of walking and talking. Mark the feeble, staggering, and awkward exhibition of that little girl in her first attempts to walk; and her half-uttered sounds, syllables, and words, as she attempts to express her rude thoughts in language. But did any mother ever make such a mistake as to scold and criticise her little daughter for tottering to fall; for her awkwardness, and the crookedness of her way; or for her stammering utterances? Never: encouragement and praise only fall from her lips. Every expression of her countenance and every word she utters indicate her excessive delight in the efforts and success of her child. She knows that all those mistakes and blunders result from weakness and inexperience, and will in due time be corrected.

Why, then, cannot that mother pursue the same course in the general management of her children? Most of their imperfections result from childish weakness, as really as in walking and talking. Let her commend their struggles to overcome temptations, and speak gently and kindly of their faults, with the assurance that time and experience will do much to correct them. Develop the good, and the evil will die out from neglect. This principle is of universal application.

Consider another point; viz., the *ac-*

tivity of children, — the only examples of "perpetual motion" yet discovered. Whence this restlessness? It comes from the earth, the air, and the sun, — the great source of vitality discoverable in animal and vegetable life. This force is "pent up" in children, and is as necessary to their vitality and growth as breathing is to their existence. It must be liberated, and for the most part in aimless activity, frolic, and mischief. Why, then, censure or punish the child for his restlessness? He has no ability to keep still, and it is an absolute wrong to attempt to repress his activity. Physical development and health, and even mental growth .and vigor, depend upon it. Parents should understand these laws, and adapt the treatment of their children to this demand of their nature. "Fun and frolic" are essential to childhood, and should be encouraged and controlled, rather than restrained and rebuked.

I have said that filial obedience is not instinctive, but the result of education. It is also true that reason and judgment are not early developed. The mother will be disappointed if she expects her child to render *spontaneous* obedience to her commands, or that he will judge correctly as to the safety or propriety of his own actions. He never judges that it is best to do what his own inclinations disapprove. He is not inclined to take medicine, and cannot be argued into the belief that it is best for him to do so. He prefers to play rather than go to school; and no amount of reasoning will convince him that he should *choose* the latter. He has formed an attachment for unsafe playmates and companions, and does not see the necessity of being removed from them. His judgment is immature and unreliable, and hence should not be appealed to in such matters. He should be entirely under parental direction and control during this forming period of life.

Nor can we expect the child to know any thing of justice, right, and duty, until he has been instructed in regard to the relations and obligations of human society. To illustrate: Two children are playing upon the floor, and find a toy which both very much desire. Each is governed wholly by his own selfish wishes, and demands that toy exclusively for himself; and a quarrel is at once inaugurated. But are these children in fault, if they have never been taught the justice, propriety, and duty of yielding to each other's wishes, and gratifying each other's desires? So it is with truthfulness. Children know nothing of the desirableness of truth-telling, or the wickedness of falsehood, unless they have been taught this important lesson. How can they know even what truth is, unless by instruction?

And what is truth to the child? He is delighted with his newly-acquired power of expressing ideas of external objects by the use of words. He comes in from his play, and says to his mother, "Me see a horse." — "No," replies the mother: "the horses are all out of doors. You don't see a horse here in the house." But he re-assures her by a repetition of his childish expression. Now, is that a falsehood? or did the child tell the truth? He did see the image of the horse formed from the reality in his own mind; and was not that a reality to him?

Further to illustrate: The little boy is about to join his brother in the yard to play, and takes with him two apples which his mother gives him, with instruction to share them with his brother. He resolves, as he goes out, to divide with him; but afterwards changes his mind, and eats both himself. When he returns from his play, his mother asks the boy if he gave his little brother the apple; and he replies that he did! And, as it was in his thought and purpose in the beginning, the statement was true. Applied to the act, it was false. But how can the child, without more instruction and experience, be expected to analyze and distinguish between these two cases, and especially when he remembers, that, only the day before, his mother told him a "bear story" that had not one word of truth in it? Indeed, what is the difference between the *imaginary* truths which children sometimes tell and the imaginary falsehoods which they hear from their parents or read in their sabbath-school books or other fiction provided for them by professional story-tellers?

This view of the subject will, at least, teach parents to deal gently and patiently with the early falsehoods of their children, which are often nothing more than the fancies of their imagination. They have no right to expect that young children will, at first, understand and feel the obligation to speak the truth, and should be all the more in earnest and faithful in impressing upon their tender minds these great moral lessons. They need instruction and encouragement more than severe rebuke or punishment. Let truthfulness be commended, and the pure principles and precepts of the Holy Bible be brought to bear upon the heart and conscience whenever any falseness and wrong has been discovered in the conduct of the child. By such means, both truth-telling and truth-loving will be inculcated, until they shall ripen into habits based upon settled principles of integrity, and shall regulate and control the life.

I will here repeat a fundamental principle in family government; viz., parental authority must be absolute. The only question touching this point, that will admit of discussion, is, What means shall be employed to establish and maintain this authority? I have argued that gentle measures, if early and wisely employed, would always accomplish the object; that dealing properly and faithfully with the *mind* and *heart* of the child would enable the parents to avoid, for the most part, the necessity of inflicting physical pain. But such wisdom and skill are not the birthright of all parents; nor are they attainable by all. Some lack the ability, others the requisite knowledge, and still others firmness, patience, and perseverance, in the use of the best methods of family government. As a consequence, insubordination reigns in many a household. Here the question returns to us, Shall parental authority be enforced? I answer, unhesitatingly, in the affirmative. It must be maintained by mildness or severity, as the occasion may demand. Taking families as we find them, corporal punishment is sometimes not only proper, but absolutely necessary; and, when such cases occur, the punishment should be adapted to the circumstances of the case, and should be promptly and faithfully administered, not as "a last resort," or "an evil to be deplored," but as an appropriate and saving remedy. It should never be inflicted in anger, but always attended and followed by kindness and sympathy. "Solomon's rod," which, if "spared," will "spoil the child," is undoubtedly a symbol of authority, as the sceptre is the symbol of power; but the right and duty to establish and maintain authority implies the right and duty to use the *literal* rod when necessary, as really as other and milder measures. Those parents accomplish the end enjoined by the precepts of Solomon who exercise complete control over their children, either with or without the infliction of bodily pain; and those who fail to govern "spoil" their children, however freely they may use the rod.

The principle here laid down is, that the parent must govern, and the child obey; and, if obedience is refused, it must be enforced. It is unfortunate that the mother, through neglect or mismanagement, has allowed her children to grow up in rudeness and insubordination; and that the father, through incapacity or want of time, has failed to retain control over them. As the result, they become more and more ungovernable in the family; will carry their turbulent spirit into the school and into society; and will, in maturer life, defy the authority of the State and the laws of God. But if such habits have been formed, and this disobedience and recklessness cannot be checked except by harsh measures, every consideration of duty as parents, and of affection and interest for the children, urges this severe course of treatment.

The amputation of a mortified limb is a terrible remedy; but it often saves life. The importance of *early* training, to secure obedience by gentle means, cannot be over-estimated; but if this duty has been neglected, and ill-temper and obstinacy in maturer life have brought these children into collision with their parents, they must be conquered and subdued.

Says the younger Edwards to a friend, —

"Remember, there is but one mode of family government. I have brought up and educated fourteen boys, two of whom I brought up, or rather suffered to grow up, without the rod. One of these was my youngest brother; the other, Aaron Burr, my sister's only son (both of them were orphans from infancy). And, from my observation and experience, I tell you, sir, 'maple-sugar government' will never answer. Beware how you let the first act of disobedience in your little boys go unnoticed, and, unless evidence of repentance be manifest, unpunished."

A practical question here urges itself upon our consideration. Shall the child be *subdued* in every instance, or punished only for disobedience, and allowed to retire without submission? If the parent has provoked the controversy, — as may be the case by some rash or unreasonable act of her own, — it may be the easiest if not the best way to solve the difficulty, to regard the act of disobedience as final, and punish for this alone, leaving the command out of the question. But there is danger in this course, even in such cases. The child has rebelled, and has been punished simply for disobedience. He has not submitted: his punishment has not subdued him. Indeed, he has virtually conquered in the contest.

The parent should avoid, with great care, every unnecessary provocation; should see to it that her commands are reasonable, and are given in the right spirit; and then she may insist upon unconditional and immediate obedience. If this is refused, she should proceed to enforce her orders, and never dismiss the case until this object is accomplished. No definite rule can be given as to the kind and degree of punishment to be inflicted in such cases: each judicious mother may settle that question for herself. The principle is unchangeable: *obedience must be rendered;* but the method of securing this result may be varied by circumstances. There are certain kinds of corporal punishment, however, which are never proper or tolerable. Among these are standing or sitting for a long time in an unnatural position, holding weights in the outstretched hand, and shaking the child by hold upon his shoulders. Such violence threatens physical injury, and therefore is wrong. When severe punishments are needed, they should be adapted to the circumstances of the offence, and inflicted promptly, deliberately, and so thoroughly that a repetition will not be called for.

VI.

CHARACTER AND HABITS.

THE character and habits of childhood are the results of family-training, and they will re-appear in manhood. Hence the great importance of parental care and solicitude as they contemplate their duty from this stand-point. The child must establish a character of integrity, and be trained to habits of honesty, benevolence, and industry, or he will be lost to himself and to society. And yet how many parents not only impart no practical lessons to aid in forming this character and these habits, but, by their own life and management, encourage dishonesty, selfishness, and indolence!

They practise deception in dealing with their children, and thus teach them to be false. They make promises which they never fulfil, threaten punishments which they never inflict, and sometimes tell their children absolute falsehoods in regard to their food, medicine, or sports. They do not realize the fact nor understand the influence of such treatment upon the heart and character of susceptible childhood; but it must be disastrous. Their own example of truthfulness should be accompanied by positive moral lessons drawn from life and from the Scriptures of truth touching this subject to enforce the precepts of honesty.

Selfishness, too, is often encouraged and cultivated under parental example. We may not expect benevolence to spring up spontaneously in the heart of the child. It is a plant of tender growth, and must be nourished by divine as well as human influence. Without knowledge and experience, the child cannot appreciate the rights and wants of others, nor his own duty in regard to them. His first attention must necessarily be directed to himself; and the natural tendency of his life is to form selfish habits. To counteract this tendency, and to cultivate the feeling and habit of benevolence, is evidently an important duty of parents. Indeed, it is through parental fidelity alone that the divine promise, "Train up a child in the way he should go, and when he is old he will not depart from it," can be realized. The evil contemplated is often the result of excessive care and indulgence. If all the wants of the child are anticipated, and every member of the household is accustomed to run at his bidding, the "little darling" will have a right to conclude that he is the most important person on the premises, and will expect and demand unlimited gratification. So indulged and gratified, the habits of self-denial and self-reliance, which are indispensable to success and happiness in life, will not be formed; nor will the ear be trained to listen to the calls of mercy and benevolence.

Harmless Indulgence.

The indulgence of children in every thing that is harmless, as I have said, is eminently proper. We have, therefore, only to distinguish between the *harmless* and *harmful*, to understand and avoid the contemplated evil. Whatever endangers life is harmful; and hence children must not be indulged in eating poison, or playing upon the margin of a precipice. Whatever endangers health is harmful;

and hence eating at improper times, in improper quantities, or of improper food, and especially of those luxuries which serve only to gratify a perverted appetite, should never be allowed. Whatever tends to deprave the moral character, or to cultivate and strengthen the selfish propensities, is harmful; and hence "evil communications," corrupting literature, and every degrading habit, should be strictly prohibited.

Our cities are thronged with young men from the country who are on the highway to ruin through want of self-restraint, and love of pleasure. And where and how were these victims of dissipation, lust, and crime, trained? I answer, In the home school of selfishness, and under the instruction of their own unwise and too-indulgent parents. The depraved appetite was there formed, and the selfish passions there cherished and indulged. Can it be possible that the seed sown in early childhood, and watered by the tears and warmed by the sunlight of parental love, has sprung up, grown, and ripened into such a fearful harvest? It is even so. The enemy "sowed tares" while the divinely ordained guardians of the home "slumbered and slept."

And vanity, another form of selfishness, is the product of early training, and more often in matters of dress. How numerous the young women of our land who have become the victims of fashion and folly; who disdain solid culture and genuine refinement; who seek their greatest enjoyment in the gay assembly, at places of amusement, and over the latest and most exciting novel; and who, with distorted views of life, judge of merit by the false standard of wealth and social position! They too often ignore superior talents and high attainments unless decked in the splendor which money can purchase. Such vanity and selfishness can plead no apology, and can find no cure. But who has distilled such wasting folly into the minds of these daughters? Was it not the mother's example and precept that first gave her little girl a fondness for dress, and an admiration for fashionable display, which, in her riper years, occupy all her time and thoughts? Children should be tastefully and neatly dressed, and should acquire a love for the beautiful in nature and art; but they should be taught, at the same time, the proper use of apparel, and the great excellence of moral and intellectual attainments to elevate and adorn female character. If properly taught and managed through the period of girlhood, they will become women who may have wealth and culture without being proud and vain; who may become fashionable in the true sense of that term, and yet judge themselves and others by the approved standard of excellence.

Emulation.

Selfishness in the child is developed also through emulation. We must here distinguish between the good and the bad in the application of this principle. Emulation that seeks excellence and distinction for their own sake, and for the advantages they bring to their possessor, is commendable. It implies a strong desire for superiority; but it has honor for its basis, and a desire for greater usefulness. Hence Dryden says with propriety, —

> "A noble emulation heats your breast."

But, when competition degenerates into rivalry, it engenders envy, resentment, and detraction, and seeks only self-gratification. The former aims to *merit* success: the latter is satisfied to *obtain* it. An appeal to this principle in the family or school usually awakens only an envious and selfish ambition. And hence the offering of prizes to the one who shall excel all others in a given task is open to serious objections. Such a prize is not a reward of *merit*, but of *success*, which is often gained through superior ability or superior advantages, and at the expense of every noble and generous feeling. This kind of emulation may secure to one or two of a class a higher order of attainments; but this is frequently gained at the sacrifice of that generous sympathy and true manliness which are the only sure guaranty of future success and usefulness. The many who have made the greater effort, and are really more deserving, are wronged, and the successful competitor is always injured more than benefited by such promotion. Pride and selfishness, under such training, soon become the ruling passion of his heart. Hence I would say to parents, as I have said to teachers, Let all prizes offered to children be based upon real merit; and let them be given to *all* the deserving, instead of *one*.

Again: selfishness sometimes degenerates into dishonesty, which manifests itself in the little business transactions among children. A favorite son, for instance, boasts that he has "got the best end of the bargain" in exchanging knives or pencils with his playmates; and his doting father smiles approvingly upon his success, and marks this act of shrewdness as evidence of special business talent. The boy has had the example, it may be, of his father and of his father's neighbors, and has observed that *overreaching* is the common habit of many in society in the transactions of every-day life; and why may he not practise sharpness, and be commended for it? If petty fraud is so common among men, why may not their sons follow their example, and learn the *art of trade* thus early? Is it strange that we so often read of theft and forgery, and peculations from government, and embezzlements from bank and railroad corporations, when so many of our youth are trained in the school of selfishness from early childhood? Whatever we desire to have expressed in the nation's life must be taught to our children both by example and precept. And what so important as strict integrity and benevolence, in distinction from dishonesty and selfishness? But these habits, also, must be formed under faithful family training, if they are to appear in practical life. They are based upon the golden rule of

Christianity, "Thou shalt love thy neighbor as thyself;" and in this loving and doing for others "there is great reward." It is not in receiving benefits from our fellow-men or from God that we experience the greatest happiness, but in laboring for their good, and in the exercise of the benevolent spirit. And this important lesson can be easily impressed upon the tender hearts of children by teaching them to share their food and playthings with each other. Unfortunate is that mother who has only *one* child to train for her country and her God; unfortunate indeed is that child who has no brothers or sisters to call forth his generous sympathies and self-denying actions. He may, on this very account, grow up a "spoiled child" through selfish indulgence. But that child who has learned this important lesson in early life may have begun a journey across the continent, or a voyage across the ocean, to carry civilization and Christianity to the destitute and needy.

INDUSTRY.

To the same end, children should be trained to habits of industry. "The idle brain is the Devil's work-shop." And this is not all: industry rightly understood and directed calls into exercise the benevolent feelings. Children should be taught to work voluntarily and cheerfully, and for the sake of helping their parents and doing good to all around them. And this helpful service may be rendered still more extensively, as opportunity offers, by *earning money*, not to be spent for their own gratification, but to enable them to contribute of their own means for the relief of suffering humanity. To forget self, and love others, is Godlike; and this is a very important lesson for childhood to learn.

How instructive the answer of our Saviour to the bigoted Jews who sought to slay him because he wrought miracles on the sabbath day! — "My Father worketh hitherto, and I work." The "Father worketh." Prompted by infinite love, he works for the welfare of his creatures; and it is only through the working of his power that his love is manifested. Christ worked to relieve the suffering poor, to comfort the afflicted, to bind up the broken heart, and to breathe into the benighted soul conscious of sin and guilt the sunlight of hope, joy, and blessedness. And he is our example. The spirit he manifested, and the lessons he taught, should be imparted to our children, that they may become co-workers with him in the world's elevation and redemption. For the want of such training, how many young men of our day are spending their lives in indolence, and wasting their energies both of body and mind in useless or ruinous indulgence! And how many young women, lost to every noble sentiment and aim in life, spend their years in the cold formalities of etiquette, in frivolous gossip among their equals, and in dressing and pleasure-seeking! Let parents, if they can, estimate the consequences of such habits to their children and to the world, and they will have a measure of their own remissness in neglecting duties so important.

Good Manners.

The family should also be a school of good manners. Manners and morals are intimately connected. One is the counterpart of the other, and both are indispensable to constitute the true man or woman. To quote an illustration which

I have employed in another work, "Morals are the basis of human character; and manners are its decorations, which serve to make it more attractive and lovely. Morals are the staple of human laws, and the regulators of human governments; and refined manners serve as gildings to make laws more effective, and government more secure." And, while I urge the necessity of training children to habits of integrity and virtue, I claim that it is also the duty of parents to give *special* attention to their manners. It is a mistaken notion that morality, or even piety, alone, will so far regulate the conduct that *social* culture will be unnecessary. How often do we have occasion to regret the lack of refinement in those whose characters we admire! and all the more do we pity them because of their generosity and goodness. Such persons would not violate the laws of good breeding, if they knew it; but, to their sorrow, they have learned that canons of etiquette are not found in creeds and codes of Christian morals. They are liable to come to our table with "dirty nails," or to "mop their foreheads" with their napkins; and yet they would be utterly ignorant that they had given offence by so doing.

Good manners must be taught in the family, both by precept and example, if we expect our children to become true gentlemen and ladies, fitted to mingle in refined society. It is not sufficient occasionally to tell them how they should behave, and to rebuke them for some grave offence. They must be trained to habits of politeness with as much care as to habits of obedience and integrity. No father would expect his son to understand practical engineering without much study and *practice.* No mother expects her daughter to become a skilful pianist without critical instruction and long-continued recitations. And how absurd to suppose that gracefulness of manners can be acquired by hearing the rules of good behavior, or reading manuals of etiquette! But many children do not enjoy even these privileges. They grow up entirely ignorant of the first principles of politeness; and, when compelled to go into society, they experience painful embarrassment in consequence of their deficiency. This is not their fault; but it is none the less the source of their torture.

In other families the theory of civility may be taught, and rudeness sometimes rebuked; and yet the laws of politeness are practically disregarded.

To illustrate: The mother goes out to make an evening call, and takes with her a little son; and she is mortified to see him standing in the hall *with his hat on*, conversing with the lady of the house; and she rebukes him severely for his rudeness. Now, if this mother had required her son to uncover his head whenever he came into *her* presence, would he have been guilty of such a mistake? The children carry their *home habits* into society. If the little daughter has been required to *practise* civility in her intercourse with the family, she will not fail to make a graceful salutation when she meets the stranger at a public party. To secure these desirable results, there must be constant home-training in the art of good behavior; and this children have a right to expect and demand of their parents. They must be taught how to enter and leave a room; how to bow, walk, turn, sit, rise; how to introduce people to each other; how to behave at the table; and, in a word, how to conduct themselves under the varied circumstances of life. Then will they be fitted for access to refined society, and to come under the influence and instruction of the wise and cultivated.

But some maintain that the cultivation of habits of courtesy tends to make children *affected;* and affectation, they say, is more offensive than awkwardness. "Children must be allowed to be *natural.*" But it is natural for some children to eat greedily, and with their knives, at the table, and entirely to neglect their superiors. Others are naturally inclined to slouch into the presence of strangers with their heads covered, to speak in a loud and boorish manner, to use the parlor as if it were a gymnasium, and to interrupt and contradict their parents when conversing with visitors. Should *such* natural habits be tolerated, or corrected? But, under faithful early training, children become civil and courteous without being affected.

Self-Reliance.

I have alluded to the importance of self-reliance as a practical habit in life. It cannot be over-estimated; nor will parents be likely to give this thought too much prominence in the training of their children.

Helplessness and dependence are conditions of infancy and childhood; but children cannot always lean upon parental arms. They must be taught self-reliance. The child, at first, has no confidence in his own ability to walk. He totters and falls because he does not trust his own strength to sustain him. Hence the mother holds his outstretched hand, and leads him to his destined goal; or he leans upon a chair by which he has learned to measure his doubtful steps.

Now, how does the mother teach her darling to walk? Not by giving him more strength, but by teaching him self-reliance. He must learn to walk by walking; and after a few trials, with proper assistance, he is left in the middle of the floor, and encouraged to come to his mother's arms. No matter if he cries for help: he must not be assisted. No matter if he tumbles: the effort will give him confidence, and this confidence will give him success. In a similar manner he must be taught to take care of his own person, to provide for his own wants, and to depend upon his own efforts for the accomplishment of every desirable object.

It is the special duty of parents to cultivate the habit of self-reliance in their children in every thing relating to active life. If they fail in this in any instance, the child's education is necessarily defective, and his future success will be doubtful.

Circumstances, however, sometimes do for children what parents have failed to do. They are born in honest poverty, and trained in the school of industry. Their straitened circumstances have compelled them to form the very habits upon which success depends. Such parents often envy their more wealthy neighbors, and lament that they cannot furnish their own children the means of personal gratification and the aid which many of their associates enjoy. But what facts does the history of these families reveal? Often the children of poverty succeed, while those reared under the influence of wealth fail. And why? I answer, Because the poor man's sons are *compelled* to form habits of industry, self-reliance, and economy, and early to shift for themselves; while those who inherit riches sometimes live in indolence and luxury which result in dissipation, or in helplessness and dependence. Our country could furnish many living illustrations of this truth. Every neighborhood, every public institution, and every profession, has its examples.

But there are noble exceptions to this rule, where children improve their easy circumstances to secure a higher degree of self-culture, and to gain a higher position in life. The necessities of poverty, if accompanied by integrity and virtue, may prove a greater blessing to a family of children than the possession of wealth; and yet the children of wealthy parents *should* be so trained in early life, that their money will not prove a temptation to indolence, but an incentive and aid to greater industry and more noble efforts.

SELF-CULTURE.

Again: self-reliance is indispensable to self-culture, which is the only condition of intellectual and moral growth. All available instruction is drawn from the child's own resources. True education is not imparted, but self-produced. It results from the exercise of the powers to be developed. And this work begins, not in the school, but in the mother's arms; and success or failure depends much upon her training. To call forth and direct the energies of mind and soul is her special work. Activity is the controlling agency, and growth and progress the sure results. Coleridge once said, "There is no standing still with the mind: if it is not rising upward to become an angel, it is sinking downward to become a devil." With what care, therefore, should this mental and moral activity be directed! The elements of true manhood and womanhood are inborn; but they can be developed only by culture. Self-help and self-reliance are both the means and the conditions of success in life. Knowledge does not spring from intuition. The mind is not merely a receptacle into which the lore of the schools can be poured, but an *activity* to cull out and appropriate whatever is valuable in books, lectures, social intercourse, and the voice of the living teacher. These rouse the intellect to action, and develop its latent energies. Now, the thought to be emphasized in this connection is, that education is a process of self-development, which should be encouraged by parents to the extent of their ability. Children should be required to do their own thinking, and to draw their own inferences. They should be told but little, but induced to discover as much as possible. They should solve their own problems, and be instructed only as to how to apply themselves to the work. Outside help weakens the power of self-instruction. It is the business of the mother and teacher to guide the intellect to its appropriate food, to awaken its appetites, and fix the attention. In this way the child may be early taught the lesson of self-reliance, and habituated to the work of successful self-culture.

Practical Life.

And our children must be trained for the practical duties of the business world. If they live, the time is not far distant when they must shift for themselves. To insure success, they must acquire habits of integrity, prudence, and economy; they must learn the value and proper uses of money, and must become self-reliant and industrious. And it is evident that home-training must be chiefly relied upon for the needed instruction and discipline. Hence the *money question*, in the management of children, may be properly discussed in this connection. Children, like older persons, desire what money will purchase; and the practical question is, To what extent and in what manner shall they be gratified? The only way for them to learn the use of money, either for their present or future benefit, is by *using* it.

How, then, shall our children be taught practically the important principles of political economy? The more common way of furnishing them money is to give only when they ask for it, and in quantities determined by the frequency and importunity of their calls. Let us inquire how this method operates in a practical way. If the boy finds that he can be gratified only through importunity and servility, he will soon lose all feelings of

delicacy and manly pride in business-matters. He will learn to gain his object through artfulness and pertinacity, and will have little inducement to take care of his money, to form plans of expenditure, or to practise self-denial. The amount to be obtained does not depend upon his frugality or financial skill, but upon his coaxing and persistency. Hence the tendency of this fitful and uncertain method of obtaining money is to foster the growth of all the ignoble propensities of the boy's nature, and to discourage the cultivation of his better qualities. I may, therefore, venture here to suggest "a more excellent way." Let parents fix upon a definite sum of money to be given to the child at stated times. It may be a weekly or monthly allowance, of such an amount as is thought best for the child to control. This should always be promptly paid, and left entirely at

the disposal of the party receiving it. Prompt payments by parents tend to cultivate the same habit in children; and giving them control of their own money enables the parents to instruct them, and to train them from their earliest years, to habits of forecast, thrift, economy, and benevolence. They must be taught to distinguish between the useful and the injurious, and encouraged to spend their money only for what is harmless or really beneficial, for their own gratification; and to contribute to the relief of the suffering and needy, remembering that "it is more blessed to give than to receive."

It is sometimes objected that this method of furnishing money to children leads them to regard these regular payments as debts, instead of gifts, from their parents, and hence they are liable to lose all feelings of obligation; but it is not necessarily so. This systematic arrangement does not prevent occasional gifts as rewards of merit, or expressions of parental affection. The object to be gained is the cultivation of correct habits in the use of money and in business-life more than the winning of affection. Besides, the bestowing of too many gifts upon children results in the cultivation of selfishness instead of love and a sense of obligation. This should be avoided.

I will here allude to a modification of the method of furnishing money to children above recommended, which may be still better. Instead of giving the money at stated periods, let parents open an account with their children, or establish a savings-bank where they can deposit their money for safe keeping. Let each one have a separate book of suitable size, and properly ruled, in which the weekly allowance is to be credited, and all sums which the child desires to draw be charged. This obviates the necessity of prompt payments, and enables children early to become acquainted with business forms, and habituated to the management of their own affairs, in a systematic manner; and after a short time, and with proper instruction, they can keep their own books, and transact their own business. In this way parents really open with their children a kind of savings-bank, encouraging them to allow to remain on interest the larger part of their income, adding interest to principal, until enough has accumulated to make some profitable investment for the distant future. Thus will something be saved, and such business habits formed as will tend to secure success in maturer life. Under proper instructions, and after limited practice, these children will need but little dictation or restraint as to the manner of spending or investing their money. They will form a correct judgment, and acquire an accuracy and self-reliance which will be invaluable to them. Better allow them to make some blunders, to be corrected, than to deprive them of the benefit of the discipline. We may be as generous as we please with our children; but all business with them should be transacted with promptness and accuracy, *in a business-like way.* Thus may we hope to prepare them for success and usefulness in riper years.

VII.

RELIGIOUS TRAINING.

THE vast importance of *religious* training for our children must not, for a moment, be lost sight of. I urge this point, not only in view of the personal relations of these children to society, but in view of their own duty and happiness in their eternal relations to God.

It is conceded by all that morality is an indispensable element in individual or national character. But, without religion, there could be no morality. Religion takes every principle, and rule of morals, under its peremptory sanction; and every pure precept which has ever been inculcated, either by infidels or Christians, has had one common origin, — the inspired word of God.

Infidelity is an element of national decay. The State could hope to gain no strength in the future from an army of children educated exclusively under its influence. Such a training could not fit them for the duties of citizenship in a Christian community, and under laws founded upon Christian principles.

The elements of a noble manhood, which develop and inspire Christian patriotism, are not inborn. Benevolence, love of truth, sobriety, and industry, spring not from inclination or habit, but result from the teachings and regenerating power of the gospel. Our youth must be educated under its influence, and imbued with its spirit, if we may hope for the prosperity and perpetuity of the republic.

The religious training of their children is the first duty of parents; and they must take this work into their own hands. So said the inspired penman when giving the Decalogue to the Jews: "And these words, which I command thee this day, shall be in thy heart; and thou shalt teach them diligently unto thy children, and shalt talk of them when thou sittest in thy house, and when thou walkest by the way, and when thou liest down, and when thou risest up."

And a still higher authority enjoins upon parents the same great duty: "Suffer little children to come unto *me*," said our Saviour. This injunction is addressed directly to all fathers and mothers to whose care have been committed "little children." Now is the time when they are to be instructed in divine things, and when they are to be suffered and directed to come to Jesus, the great

Teacher and Guide of sinful men. Their minds are just opening to understand the visible and invisible things which are revealed; their hearts are now tender and susceptible of durable impressions; and their growing life is waiting, as it were, to be directed by the loving hand of the mother into the path of duty, peace, and usefulness.

The personal welfare of our children recurs for our consideration. A life of virtue and piety stands opposed to a life of vice and crime. The former is a life of happiness; the latter, of misery. The one leads to honor and usefulness; the other, to disgrace and ruin. And no right-minded parent can be indifferent as to which of these paths his children tread. Vital interests are involved in this question, when contemplated only from a worldly stand-point; and when we admit the doctrine of a future and endless life, of which the present is but an introduction, and for which it is a preparation, the subject assumes a fearful importance. The duty of parents, in obedience to the divine injunction, to teach the great truths of Christianity diligently unto their children, now becomes imperative and imposing.

And what truths of Christianity are so important for our children to understand? I answer, first of all, that great truth in subordination to which all the moral precepts of the Decalogue are proclaimed; viz., that there is one, and only one, great First Cause, who is the source of all human obligations, and the only object of human worship. This is the foundation of all revealed truth. Without it human life is a desert, shut in on every side by an impenetrable horizon. Without this truth, man knows nothing of his origin, and nothing of his end. Let parents, therefore, teach this to their children, with all the accompanying precepts, so well calculated to regulate human conduct and inspire human hopes.

And "suffer" the little children to come to Jesus, the perfect exemplification of all religious truth. Send them not to the schools of the Pharisees to learn lessons of morality, dogmas, and creeds, but to Him "who teaches as never man taught." Induce them to imitate his example, obey his precepts, and cherish his spirit, and they will attain to a higher morality, a purer life, and more exalted joys, than human philosophy has ever taught. The yearning tenderness which has flowed from the words and deeds of Christ towards "little children" is well calculated to call forth their love, and win them to obedience.

The truth of God's existence and attributes can be impressed upon the minds of children by directing their attention to the visible creation. The starry heavens above them speak of his goodness, wisdom, and power; the wide expanse of living verdure, fertile fields, shady groves, and blooming gardens, express his constant love and bountiful care. All Nature proclaims a God, and invites us to reverence and adore.

Instruction in these great truths must be drawn from the Holy Bible. We can direct our children to no other fountain, can give them no other guide of life, and can point them to no other Saviour, than is herein revealed. Here are unfolded the institutions of the gospel, the means of grace, and every duty that man owes to his fellow-man and to God. It is our special duty, therefore, as parents, to impress upon their tender minds the pure principles drawn from these sacred pages.

But children must be dealt with as

children. They should not be so introduced to the theory and practice of Christian principles and observances as to be repelled and disgusted: they should be allured to the delightful paths of virtue and piety.

They cannot comprehend the unmeaning technicalities of religion; and hence parents should not read to them homilies on Christian ethics or systematic theology. The truth must be opened to their minds through their own channels of thought and action. Childhood must be *amused.* Its innocent sports are its very life and activity; and, as intimated in another connection, this activity is the only condition of its development and growth. Children, therefore, in their freedom, and in the use of their toys, obey an imperative law of their being. The question is, How far in their religious culture should they be restrained? The sabbath was made for children as well as for men and women. But was it designed to abridge their freedom, and cut off all their enjoyments? Must all their books and toys be laid aside, and they be subjected to a formal service for which they have no taste, and in which they can now take no pleasure? If so, the sabbath will become a burden, to be anticipated with dread, and endured with impatience, and all its beneficial influence worse than lost to these children. It must follow, therefore, if parents would bring their children under a wholesome religious influence, they must make the sabbath a delight; must adapt its duties to their nature; and select and control their amusements, instead of suppressing them. The Divine Master delights to see "little children" happy on the sabbath as well as on week-days; and must approve of their freedom and childish glee, if only it can be tempered and sweetened by a holy religious influence. I will not presume to specify as to how these desirable results can be secured, but would earnestly enjoin upon all parents who seek the religious welfare of their children, as far as possible, to make the principles and precepts of our holy religion pleasant and attractive to them. "And, ye fathers, provoke not your children to wrath; but bring them up in the nurture and admonition of the Lord;" remembering that they who bequeath to their children the results of a thorough Christian education endow them with riches more valuable and enduring than silver and gold.

VIII.

INTELLECTUAL CULTURE.

"'Tis education forms the common mind:
Just as the twig is bent, the tree's inclined."

THOSE parents make a grave mistake who rely solely upon the public school for the mental training of their children. This discipline should begin early at home, and under the most careful supervision. As soon as the child opens his eyes and puts forth his little hands, as soon as his senses come in contact with the material world, the mind begins to drink in knowledge, and expand by means of its own activity. The foundations of the man's education are laid mainly in the home of his childhood, and before he has reached the proper school-age. Faithful *early* home-training is, therefore, of the utmost importance.

"Just as the *twig* is bent, the tree's inclined."

Neglect or improper instruction in childhood may result in waste and failure in riper years. The "twig" must be *properly* "bent," that the tree may be developed in symmetrical and stately proportions. The growth of the tree results from its own vitality; but the shape and direction of its trunk and limbs depend upon its trimming and training. So also in education. Self-culture is the only means of sound mental development; but this must be inspired, directed, and controlled, during childhood, by parental fidelity and wisdom.

And first of all, and mainly, home-training should consist in the discipline of the observing faculties. Books are little needed at this period, except so far as they may aid in directing attention to the real objects by which the child is surrounded, and in explaining their qualities and uses. The mind of the child opens upon a world of objects, and his education must impart mainly *object*-lessons.

A thirst for knowledge is inherent in every human mind, and is *early* manifested. The child observes, and soon learns to distinguish his friends and benefactors from strangers. He watches with intense interest every motion that comes within range of his vision; he grasps every solid object placed within his reach, — the watch, the pencil, the knife, the toy, — and bears it to his mouth, seemingly to make more sure the knowledge of its peculiar properties by the aid of two senses at once; and, as soon as this child has gained the power of locomotion, he goes in search of objects to the extreme limit of his little dominion. When the power of speech is gained, he hastens to call every thing by its proper name, and to ask endless questions as to its nature and utility.

Here, then, is the parent's opportunity to commence the work of education. First, it is the instructor's duty to remove from reach and sight, as far as possible, all objects which the child may not handle; secondly, to select such toys for the child's use as are proper and the most interesting; and, finally, to be ready to answer all inquiries, and to impart such instruction as each subject will admit. Another important thought in this connection, — the child should have the earnest sympathy of the parent in all his efforts to gratify curiosity and gain knowledge, in all his sports and games. The parent should give attention when the child, delighted, holds up his new-found treasure: he should smile upon his expressed enthusiasm, and encourage his search for truth. Kind looks and gentle words have a magic power over the mind of childhood under such circumstances.

Among the first practical lessons to be imparted in the examination of the objects which occupy the attention of the child are the names, parts, qualities, and uses of these objects. For illustration, take the object *dinner-bell*, with which every child is familiar. What are its parts? It has a handle, tongue, and chain. What are its qualities? It is hard, smooth, and sonorous. What are its acts? It rings, strikes, and sounds. What are its uses? It calls to dinner. *A sheet of paper* is another object. Its parts? It has ends, edges, surface, and lines. Its qualities? It is smooth, limber, and pliable. Its uses? To write and print upon, and make books.

Next we may call attention to the idea of number, form, size, color, and weight. For example, take the object *cat.* The number? one. Its size? large. Its form? that of a quadruped. Its color? black. Its weight? ten pounds. Its qualities? it is hairy, smooth, playful, cunning. Its use? it is good to catch mice. Again: let *boy* be the object. The number? many. Form? like a man. Size? small. Color? white. Weight? thirty pounds.

The idea of size, measurement, and weight, is determined by comparison with a unit of measure; and accuracy in measuring with the eye is acquired only by practice. Then give the child a measure, and teach him its use; drill him, at every opportunity, to judge of the bulk and distance of objects around him; the size and weight of a stone; the length, breadth, and height of the table, the bureau, or the room itself; accustom him to distinguish the colors of the different objects that meet his eye, and the various sounds that greet his ear.

Parents may next open to their children the book of Nature, and trace with them its ample pages. What a fruitful field for mental culture and refinement is here spread out before them! — the heavens above, with their rolling planets and shining stars; the dew that collects upon the grass; the gently-falling rain that distils from the clouds; the frost, ice, and snow which appear in their season; the storm which gathers among the mountains, roaring and flashing with terrific thunder and forked lightnings, and pouring itself in deluging torrents upon the valleys below; the ever-changing seasons, which give "seed-time and harvest," and come freighted each with its own pleasures and blessings. What objects and themes for youthful contemplation! What sources of instruction, if the inquiring mind of childhood is properly directed!

The child in the flower-garden may take numberless lessons in discriminating colors and odors, and in learning the names and characteristics of the different flowers that adorn the landscape and delight the senses. He may cultivate a taste for the beautiful in Nature, and a fondness for that rich science which opens at this point into the wide world of vegetable creation. The child in the cultivated field should learn to distinguish between the different grasses and grains. Each kind has its own peculiar stalk and leaf, and blossom and seed. The clover-field differs from the herds-grass; the wheat, from the barley, oat, and rye-field; and, after the harvest, the kernels all differ from each other. Now, how many in the schools are put upon the study of the higher English classics and ornamental branches who are profoundly ignorant of the most common and useful facts by which their childhood was surrounded! And yet all these facts might have been known perfectly, and much profitable discipline secured, had the parents done their duty, and early called their attention to the object-lessons of Nature in the garden and in the field.

The child in the orchard and in the wood should be taught early to name, at sight, the apple, pear, peach, and plum trees; the beach, birch, and maple, with their various species; and the evergreens, which defy the chilling blasts and icy grapple of winter. He should know them by the color of their bark, and shape of their leaves, and the taste of their fruit; and he should understand their comparative utility for the purposes of food, fruit, and lumber. A knowledge of such facts would lead the young pupil to inquire into the philosophy of the vegetable world; to study the relations of the plant and the tree to the elements which surround them; and, finally, to investigate the process by which plants grow under the influence of heat, light, and moisture.

Still further: the child on the farm, among the minerals, may be profitably employed in learning the nature of the soil, and the names of the different rocks and metals with which he is familiar. The different soils, and their adaptation to the different crops which the farmer expects them to yield; the manner of enriching and cultivating them; the times and seasons for casting the seed, nursing the plants, and gathering the harvest, — are facts every boy should understand; and the girl, the corresponding facts in her own domestic department.

The difference between the common metals, — iron, lead, copper, silver, and gold, — their uses and comparative values, and the localities from which they are obtained; why gold is more valuable than silver, and silver than copper, and copper than lead, when used as coin; and why iron is the most valuable of all metals when used in the arts, — are facts which every child can and should understand, even while in the home school of Nature. A knowledge of these facts will lead to the science of agriculture, housekeeping, mineralogy, geology, and lay the foundation for a successful business-life.

And, finally, the child may be introduced to the animal world. Domestic animals first attract his attention. They become his companions and his delight. The dog, the cat, the cow, the horse, are watched and trained and enjoyed in the pastime of every-day life. The first business of the parent is, therefore, to teach the child the distinctive nature and habits of these animals. This instruction will tend to awaken a new interest in the whole subject of animal existence, and will lead the young learner to study the history of the *wild* animals that roam our forests and occupy other countries. From a knowledge of the domestic fowls that afford the child so much pleasure, he learns to listen with delight to the songs of the birds which frequent the groves about his dwelling, and to study with interest their varying forms, colors, notes, habits, and history; and ere long, under proper encouragement, he is ready to search the whole field of natural history for new objects of interest.

And home instruction in the animal kingdom finds an endless variety of objects in the department of insects.

They fill the air we breathe, the water we drink, and every foot of soil upon which we tread. In species they are countless, in variety almost infinite. Now, the child is familiar with many of these short-lived but evidently happy little creatures. Give him a microscope, and teach him to study with care their habits and history.

The water also teems with its own inhabitants: the finny tribes and the shell-fish are all objects of great interest and profit for home lessons and instruction.

Home geography affords another appropriate subject for home mental culture. Children should have their attention directed early to the prominent facts on this important subject. First, they may be taught the points of compass, — east, west, north, and south. These will be more easily and correctly fixed in the mind by observing the position and direction of the sun. Let the child take a stand-point facing that luminary at the time of its rising. The sun is now in the east; and the opposite point is due west. Now let him stretch out his arms, and point his fingers, and his left hand will point to the north, and his right hand to the south. This practical lesson, learned from observation, should now be applied to directions of different objects in the room and in the field. The sides of the room — which is east, west, north, and south? What direction is the stove from the opposite window, and the window from the stove? What is the direction of the church, the schoolhouse, and the store, from the house? Does the street run north and south? or east and west? Which way does the brook or river run? and which way do the clouds move?

Next the attention of the child may be directed to "a description of the earth;" that is, the door-yard with which he is familiar; the field, the pasture, and the wood, over which he roams. He should be taught to observe the hills and the vales, the rocks and the trees and the streams, and be required to describe them in his childish way. He should "bound" the yard, the field, and the farm, carefully observing the points of compass and the portions of land, or neighboring farms adjoining. And, with the points of compass, he should be taught distances and measurements; the number of rods in the garden-fence, and to a neighbor's house; the number of miles to the next village; the number of acres in the cornfield and meadow. Such instruction lays the foundation for that thorough and practical knowledge which enabled Columbus to discover a continent, and which is important in every department of life.

The observing faculties are early exercised also in numbering the different objects which come in childhood's way; and this is practical arithmetic. Counting the fingers was the origin of the Arabic and Roman methods of notation, the reason of the increase from right to left by *tens*, and of the *ten* characters which we have to represent numbers. Hence the word *digits*, the name (from *digiti*) given to the figures; which literally means *fingers*.

Let children be put to counting their fingers, their blocks, their marbles, the doors and windows with their panes of glass, and the sets of household articles. Let them count the flocks and herds, the stones and trees, and all the objects of Nature which can attract their attention. Let them count the stars, "which no man can number." They should also be required to exercise their memory by recalling the things they have counted; to exercise their judgment by considering comparative bulk in relation to numbers: and, to make this home instruction practical, let counting, adding, and subtracting be applied to the business transactions of the farm, the workshop, and the store.

By the proper discipline of the observing faculties in childhood, two desirable objects will be accomplished, which cannot fail to have an important bearing upon the success and welfare of the man and woman in after-life. First, a taste will be cultivated, and a foundation laid, for accurate and successful study in the different departments of science, literature, and language. This *home* school is necessary to fit the child for the different grades of instruction which he will receive in the public school, academy, and college.

The second object to be secured by training the eye and ear to accurate seeing and hearing is the habit of knowing and telling the truth. Careless observation must result in imperfect knowledge and false representation. Misapprehensions, and misstatements of facts, are, to-day, prevailing evils in every neighborhood and in every grade of society in our land. The gossip of the "tea-party" and the gossip of the newspaper continue to disturb the peace of every community by manufacturing strife and stirring up scandal. History and literature are full of misreprentations, and the whole nation is groaning under a burden of *lies.* And who can fail to see that one fruitful source of these evils may be found in the neglect of early training, as above specified?

A practical question here arises: How shall the habit of accurate observation be formed in childhood? I answer briefly: Encourage the child to observe, with fixed attention, every thing and every occurrence that meets his senses. Then, as a test of this accuracy, require a description of what has been seen or heard. For instance: The mother is about to spread the table, and furnish it for a tea-party. She requires her little girl to sit down and watch every movement until her work is accomplished; and then she will be expected to give a full account of every step in the process, in its order and in full, even to the number of the plates, cups and saucers, knives and forks and spoons, which have been used. Or this mother wishes to send her boy on an errand. She gives him the message; but, before allowing him to start, she requires him to repeat her order again and again, until he has fixed every particular in his mind. Had the father who sent his son to a neighbor's house, to borrow a flour-barrel for the purpose of confining his puppy, taken this course, he would not have been mortified by learning the next day that his boy asked the neighbor for "an empty barrel of flour to make a dog a hen-coop."

Direct the attention of the child to the phenomena of Nature; train him to observe accurately the *time* as indicated by the watch, the clock, and especially the sun, so that he may know the hours, as they pass, by observation, and acquire the habits of promptness and industry; teach him the importance of "order," which is "heaven's first law;" and do not forget that a correct judgment cannot be formed without a full knowledge of the facts and principles, and processes of reasoning, which have a bearing upon the subject, and that these can be gained only by accurate observation and study.

But intellectual culture at home should not partake of the form and necessary strictness of school discipline. This would defeat the very object in view. Children will not bear such confinement; and would, by formal and constant requirements, acquire a distaste for the instruction to be imparted. Home-lessons should be made agreeable and attractive: and, to this end, they should be made, in a measure, optional; to be sought rather than enforced. By skilful management on the part of parents, the curiosity and interest of children may be excited, and all the desirable results secured, on the voluntary principle.

The conversation of the breakfast-table, at dinner, and at tea, should be conducted with a view to secure the improvement of our children. Little ears are always open to listen, and little minds always active to digest ideas upon interesting topics so presented. The taste is thus cultivated, the intellect expanded, and directed into the right channels of thought.

Another suggestion in this connection: When practicable, the parent should take his child with him on short excursions, and even on a journey. Nothing is better calculated to open and expand the mind than the constantly-varying scenery and circumstances which such excursions afford.

But caution should always be exercised lest parents should *over-train* and *over-task* their young children. The laws of physical as well as mental development demand that *home* life should be comparatively *free* and *active;* and yet, under wise and judicious management, it may be the season for great improvement, and for laying the foundation of a thorough, practical education, such as will develop true manhood and womanhood.

IX.

THE CHILDREN AT SCHOOL.

THE school is an expansion of the family. Children from different homes are brought together, and committed to the care and instruction of teachers employed for this purpose. These teachers occupy the place of parents; receive from them delegated authority and power; and assume their duties for the purpose of carrying forward and completing the important work of education. This work, as we have seen, does not begin with the school; nor is it confined to the study of books. It begins with infancy, under the influence of the mother's smiles and tears and anxious care; it progresses through childhood, in the midst of toys, and a world of *objects* which address themselves to the senses, and interest the mind, of the little stranger. These are the most important periods of life, as the child now receives the most durable impressions, and forms the most lasting habits. But the time at length comes when parental inability, or absorbing home cares and toils, forbid proper attention to the child's higher education. Assistance must be secured. The school becomes a necessity; but by no means, and at no time, should our children be committed *entirely* to the care of others. It is an hour of special peril, when without experience, or practical knowledge of the world, they are sent out to mingle with new associates, to form new relations, and to come under new control. There is need, therefore, of greater parental vigilance and fidelity than ever before. No greater mistake can be made than to suppose that the discipline of the family may be confined to the home, and that parental responsibility ceases when public instruction begins. This discipline and watchfulness and special care should extend over the whole period of minority.

I come now, therefore, to consider the practical questions which have a bearing upon the relations of parents to the schools in which their children are educated.

At What Age

should children be sent to the public school? From *four* to *eighteen* is the ordinary legal school-age. Some foolish mothers send their children to school even earlier than the law suggests, to get them out of the way. They have the "babies" still at home to be cared for, but do not realize that the teacher, with twenty, thirty, or forty pupils to govern and instruct, has no time to give attention to their restless children who are too young to be instructed at the school.

But they ought to know that the school-room is no place for so young children. Such an imprisonment, with nothing to do, is an absolute wrong and injury to the little prisoners. They have committed no crime; and they need and have a right to claim the freedom of home, with their toys and pets and sports. The activity which such freedom alone can secure is absolutely necessary for healthy physical development. Besides, the *object*-teaching and self-culture of the home-school are far better for the child than the false system of primary instruction adopted in most of our public schools.

Another thought in this connection:

When sent to school too early, and improperly taught, the child becomes disgusted with school-life, and receives an irreparable injury, affecting his progress and improvement in later years. If he enters at the right age, and is taught in the proper way, he will learn to love his school, and will acquire a taste for books and study. He must not, therefore, be sent too early. But at what age should he enter the public school? I answer, Better at *twelve* than three years old, better at *eight* than *five*, and never younger than *six;* and, if the school which he must attend is decidedly poor, he should be delayed still longer.

I have urged the importance of correct primary instruction at home, and have here alluded to the importance of adopting the same system in the school. This is Nature's method, — the *object* first, and then the *sign*, which may be either a *pic-*

ture or a *word;* and, in either case, it should be seen and recognized by its looks. By this method, children are taught to read words and sentences before they know the letters of the alphabet, just as they have, at home, learned to distinguish different objects by sight and by name without stopping to analyze or explain. The analysis will come naturally afterwards, and the instruction so given will be much more interesting and profitable.

Parents as well as teachers should understand that the old system of instruction in primary schools is unnatural and unwise; and they should always give the preference, in employing instructors, to those who have been trained in *modern* methods.

Indeed, all parents should be so well informed as to the best methods of school government and instruction as to be qualified to exercise an intelligent supervision over the training of their children. Intelligence in school-matters is a necessary qualification to enable parents to appreciate a good school and a good teacher, to adopt the best system, to provide a suitable outfit, and to secure a wise administration of educational affairs.

Another practical question to consider, in preparing the public school for their children, is, What

System of Organization

shall be adopted?

Except in the cities, the *district* system has generally prevailed in this country. Every one who has given the matter any attention is aware of the disadvantages of this system; and many earnest efforts have been made to remove the evil by a change to what is termed the *town* system.

In some States, the town system has been established by law; in others, enabling acts have been passed *allowing* the towns to abolish the *district*, and establish the *town* system.

The advantages of the town over the district system may here be considered.

1. Under town supervision, the schools would all be of the same length, giving the children in every family an equal amount of instruction: under district supervision, the length of the different schools varies from twelve to thirty-six weeks during the year. And as all parents are taxed equally, according to their ability, to support the public schools, and as every man is interested in the education of every other man's children, all should enjoy equal school advantages.

2. Under town supervision, just so many schools would be established as are needed, and no more. Under the district

system, the number of schools is determined by old district lines, without regard to the number of pupils to be provided for. The result is, some of these schools are crowded much beyond the capacity of the buildings to accommodate, and others are so small that the advantages of classification and class emulation are entirely lost. And other evils result indirectly from the same cause. The small schools are likely to employ teachers of a lower grade; to have a more *stingy* outfit, and a less careful supervision.

3. Under the town system, the aggregate expenses of common schools would be much diminished. As at present managed, much money is wasted in building schoolhouses, employing teachers, and in running the schools. I have in mind an instance which will illustrate. There were in the town of L. five schools, in all

of which there were only thirty-six pupils. In *one* other school, in the same town, there was the same number. Now, the *one* school was not too large to be profitable: indeed, it could be managed to much better advantage by a single teacher than the small school of *seven* pupils. This large school was in session twenty-nine weeks during the year under review, at an expense of $260. The five small schools, running the same number of weeks, with less efficient management and less satisfactory results, cost $2,430. This gives us the practical solution in figures which "do not lie." In the large school, the whole expense of twenty-nine weeks' schooling was $7.22 for each pupil: in the small schools for the same time, the actual expense, as estimated in the town report, was $67.50 per scholar. This estimate does not include the interest on the additional amount of school property invested in the five districts compared with the one.

4. Under town supervision, more skilful teachers can be employed, and better furnished schoolhouses provided, and hence much more profitable schools secured. We cannot expect that a district of only two or three families having children to educate will be willing to incur the expense of building a new schoolhouse, and paying high salaries to their teachers.

But, under the town system, all the children in town would be provided for *equally*, and those in the rural districts would enjoy equal advantages with those in the large villages. This would be an important point gained, and would result in establishing good schools in the place of poor ones throughout the town and state.

5. The crowning advantage resulting from town supervision would be the establishment of a graded school of high order in the centre of the town, which would be accessible to all. This school would have three departments, — the *primary*, the *intermediate*, and the *academic*, — and would afford excellent facilities for every grade of pupils fitting for business and for college. Such a town system of public schools would supplant the common mixed academies, leaving only a few classical schools of high order, and the higher seminaries and colleges, where the graduates of the graded town-schools could finish their education.

6. More complete supervision of the schools would be secured under the town system. The town board of education would naturally be composed of cultivated and efficient men, and would act in concert for the common good of all.

They would not only examine, but employ, the teachers; and hence would be able to secure those who are the best qualified and adapted to the different grades of the several schools.

These are some of the many advantages which would result from abolishing the district and establishing the town system. The utility of the change has been demonstrated both in town and state where the experiment has been tried. That will be a fortunate day for the cause of education when this true system of public instruction shall have been everywhere established; and it is the first duty of parents to demand and secure the school system here recommended.

The importance of the

Graded System of Schools,

wherever such a classification can be

effected, justifies a special plea in its behalf. "A graded school," says Wells, "is a school in which the pupils are divided into classes according to their attainments, and in which all the pupils of each class attend to the same branches of study at the same time."

The special utility and desirableness of this system will occur to every intelligent mind. Let us examine it.

In a thoroughly graded school, perfect classification can be effected. Pupils of the same age, having a common interest and mutual sympathy, are brought together. The influence of class pride and emulation is brought to bear upon them. With fewer classes, more time is given for class-recitation and personal drill, and a more complete supervision of the school is secured.

Under this system, school trustees can select teachers adapted and fitted for their own special departments, and can employ them permanently; can provide a uniformity of text-books, and secure more punctuality and regularity of attendance.

None of these advantages can be realized in the mixed, unclassified school; and still this is the condition of a large majority of the public schools in every State in the Union.

These schools are thoroughly *mixed:* all children of school-age — "from four to eighteen" — are huddled together. They are provided with text-books of every kind, and upon every subject; and the teacher is expected to govern and instruct this heterogeneous assemblage in the most approved manner.

But how can she do this? There can be no system or order in such a school. Every thing is at the mercy of circumstances. There are at least three schools (in one) to be managed and taught,—the primary, the intermediate, and the academic; and still there is only *one* day at a time to be devoted to them all. The teacher must keep order, adapting her discipline to the child of *four* years, and to the man or woman of *eighteen*. A little world, with all the diversities of age and disposition, is under her administration; and for their improvement and culture she is held responsible. From twenty to thirty important recitations must be conducted daily, and at such times as chance may dictate. What can even a good teacher accomplish under such circumstances? What right have parents to expect satisfactory results from schools so organized?

The graded system secures such a division of labor as will obviate all these difficulties, and enable the teacher to bring order out of confusion, and light out of darkness.

Every one understands the importance of this principle as applied to the departments of industry in practical life. Division of labor is indispensable to success in the arts, as taught in political economy.

To illustrate, I will refer to some examples.

In the manufacture of *pins*, ten men are actually employed for the purpose of securing the benefits of classification of the different kinds of labor.

One man draws out the wire; another straightens it; a third cuts it; the fourth sharpens the point; the fifth grinds it at the top for receiving the head; and the other five men are employed in making the different parts of the head, and finishing the whole. Now, why not require each one of these ten men to make his share of the pins, independent of his fellows? I answer, No one could acquire the necessary skill and adaptation to every part of the work: much time would be wasted in passing from one point to another, and hence comparatively little would be accomplished. It is stated upon good authority that these same ten men, who, with the proper division of labor, make *forty-eight thousand* pins per day, could make only *two hundred* in the same time if each was required to perform every part of the work.

And, in the process of making a *watch*, we are told that there are *one hundred and two* distinct branches, which may employ as many different apprentices. Each one of these departments constitutes a separate trade; and the *watch-finisher* is the only man of the whole who knows how to make a watch in all its parts.

This same principle is applied to the mechanic arts generally. In all our factories, each operative has his own special department, and confines himself to the work assigned. The result is, much more efficiency and skill, and hence more productiveness of labor.

And what I here maintain is, that this division of labor should be applied to the management and instruction of our schools.

First, secure as perfect a classification of the pupils in the district as may be, according to their age and attainments; second, assign to each department a teacher who has been thoroughly trained, and is adapted especially to the position to be occupied and the work to be done; and, thirdly, furnish that teacher with the necessary books and apparatus, — tools to work with, — and the process of education will be successfully carried on.

Having settled the system of school-organization to be adopted, parents should proceed to make careful and thorough preparation for the school.

School-Sites and Schoolhouses

demand their first attention. The location of the schoolhouse is a matter of vital importance. Too often do we find it situated in some dark alley, or on some noisy street, on low and marshy ground, or upon the barren rock where no shade-trees can grow, or upon the dusty corner where four roads meet. In such localities children are disturbed by noises, suffer from excessive heat and cold, or from dampness, insufficient light, and bad air; and are robbed of all the advantages and pleasures of pleasant surroundings and tasteful arrangements of well-ordered playgrounds.

Other things being equal, the schoolhouse should have a central location, for convenience of access. But this is not the most important consideration. The character of the grounds and surroundings should weigh against a few rods of additional distance for the children to travel. The school-yard should be selected, laid out, and graded, with a view to furnish the children pleasant and attractive play-grounds. This is as important for the purposes of education as a well-constructed and well-furnished schoolroom. This yard should contain, at least, a half-acre of level or sloping ground, and should be ornamented with shade-trees, and furnished with swings, ball-bats, foot-balls, and other inducements to healthful exercise.

In selecting the site, special regard should be had to the surroundings. Noisy mills, factories, and work-shops, in the immediate vicinity of the school-house, are a serious hinderance to successful study. Stores, railroad-stations, and taverns are liable to consume the time, vitiate the taste, and corrupt the morals, of pupils who are allowed to resort to them. Hence the schoolhouse should, if possible, be removed from all such local disadvantages; and, for the sake of health, equal care should be taken to avoid stables, sewers, marshes, stagnant bodies of water, and low and damp situations where heavy fogs linger long after sunrise, and chill night-dews gather before sunset.

And the school-site should be a beautiful location, where Nature has displayed her romantic wildness and quiet grandeur. Children are taught unconsciously by the objects that surround them; and hence the place where they are gathered for the study of books should also afford opportunity for them to study the book of Nature. They should be able to gaze upon the towering mountain, the peaceful valley, the shaded forest, and the cultivated field; and to listen to the music of running brooks, and the songs of the birds that frequent the shade-trees under which they play.

The pleasantness and attractiveness of the location and surroundings of the schoolroom serve to make school-life pleasant, and to cultivate a taste for the beautiful in nature and art, — both extremely desirable as means to the end in view.

Schoolhouses should not only be properly located, but constructed with great care. Under the town system which has been here recommended, the town school board would have all these matters in hand; and they should see to it that the site is well chosen, and that each house is adapted, in size and finish, to the number and grade of the pupils to be accommodated.

The room for the primary department will need different internal arrangements from the intermediate, and the intermediate from the academic. The benches must be of suitable height to enable each pupil to rest his feet upon the floor, and so inclined as to allow a natural and easy posture; the desks must be constructed to suit the size and convenience of their occupants; and all schoolhouses should have rooms especially for hats, bonnets, shawls, overcoats, umbrellas, dinner-baskets, &c., that the children may acquire the habits of neatness and order, and learn to take care of whatever is intrusted to them.

Recitation-rooms should be furnished with blackboards and brushes, and an ample supply of apparatus suited to the character of the school: if a primary school, apparatus especially suited to illustrate object-teaching.

Lighting and heating the schoolhouse is of the first importance. Light is necessary to health; and a good supply of pure sunlight, controlled by shutters and curtains, is needed, not only for healthful study, but also to render the schoolroom more cheerful and inviting. The common mode of heating schoolrooms is very objectionable, — much more so than the old method by the open fireplace. The tight box-stove, without the means of evaporating water, in a room not suited to the purposes of ventilation, is the worst and most dangerous arrangement that could be invented. It creates an uneven temperature, deadens the air, and fills it with smoke, rendering it wholly unsuitable for the purposes of life. It is believed that more cases of fatal disease are contracted in the unventilated and improperly-heated schoolrooms of the present day than anywhere else; and it becomes a matter of great importance to all parents, who seek to prepare their children for a long and useful life, to understand this subject, and to provide against the evils contemplated.

The subject of

SCHOOLHOUSE VENTILATION

is so important to the welfare of the children in our schools, that I may properly dwell upon it for a few moments. No fact is more evident, even to common observation, than that pure air is indispensable to health; and yet there are but comparatively few schoolhouses in any community in which pure air can be breathed for three hours during a winter's day.

Modern methods of heating schoolrooms, already alluded to, have added much to the evils resulting from almost universal neglect in the matter of ventilation. The facts before us are alarming.

We may give our children the hard fare at home which were the common *rations* of other days, we may provide for them the hard benches and uncomfortable arrangements of old-fashioned schoolhouses, if we will give them also the fresh air therein provided by loose windows and spacious open fireplaces. But we cannot, without guilt, shut them up for six hours each day in a small, tight room warmed by a close box-stove. Such an atmosphere poisons the blood, drains the vitality, and lays the foundation of a hundred forms of sickness and suffering. Without pure air, the circulation of the blood, instead of a current of life, becomes a current of death, diffusing itself through a million of channels into every part of the system. Would parents buy a solution of arsenic at the druggist's, and inject it into the veins of their children? This would prove no more fatal than to inhale the poison of bad air which they are compelled to breathe in most of our schoolhouses, day after day, and week after week. The only difference is, one is a rapid and the other is a slow process of poisoning.

When the schoolroom is first opened, the air is comparatively pure: but, in a short time, the fifty pairs of lungs have consumed nearly all the oxygen; and the vicious compound that remains stupefies the intellect, and, by slow degrees, saps the very life-blood. These statements are not theory, but facts; the evils resulting are not imaginary, but real, as illustrated in the history of a large majority of the public schools in our country.

But how can this evil be removed? I answer, Only by making special provision for the circulation of fresh air in every schoolroom. Perfect ventilation cannot be secured except by scientific arrangements in connection with heating the apartments. The circulation of the atmosphere is effected through the agency of heat; and when the building is so finished as to admit a constant supply of fresh air from without, and to eject that which is impure, through ventilators prepared near the top and bottom of the upright ceiling, heat becomes the controlling power to keep the current in circulation. In the absence of any special arrangements of this kind, resort must be had to open doors and windows. These, used skilfully by parties who understand the laws of health and life, will, in a measure, secure the object in view. Yet there is danger in trusting a matter of such vital importance to arrangements so imperfect, and circumstances so variable.

I wish here to call special attention to another point which has been alluded to in this connection; viz., the importance of

SCHOOL-APPARATUS

to enable the teacher to work successfully.

Apparatus is designed to illustrate and enforce the principles of science; and its great utility is seen in the well-established fact, that instruction communicated through the sense of sight is much better understood, and much longer remembered. The child *sees* the representation of number on his "numeral frame;" he *sees* the shape of the earth in the artificial globe, and is able to trace out the ranges of mountains, the courses of rivers, and the figure of continents, upon the outline-maps which hang before him; and he understands the definition of a cube in distinction from a square surface when he *sees* and handles the block which bears that name.

Every schoolroom should have a black-board as long as the unoccupied space between the windows on every side. This will enable the teacher to represent to the eye many objects and subjects which would otherwise be either lost or imperfectly understood by the pupils; and will enable them to solve the problems in the presence of the class and teacher, greatly to their benefit.

No schoolroom is perfectly furnished which has not in it a thermometer, to enable the teacher to regulate the temperature; and an unabridged dictionary of the English language is indispensable, to be consulted daily and hourly by the whole school as they prosecute their studies.

Thorough instruction cannot be given without these helps; and the more advanced departments should be provided with a cabinet, library and philosophical apparatus, more or less extensive as circumstances require.

Having settled the system of school-organization to be adopted, and having provided a suitable schoolhouse favorably located and well furnished, the next important duty to be performed by parents is to select and employ a

Highly Competent Teacher.

Under the district-system, this duty devolves upon the school-trustees selected for that purpose. Under the town-system, which I have earnestly commended, it belongs to a committee of the town-board of education. In either case, it is a question of vital importance who are to be intrusted with the management and instruction of our schools.

The education of the young prince or

princess, in royal governments, is regarded as an important matter, affecting, as it must, the welfare of nations. The selection of a tutor for such an heir to the throne always excites a deep interest and solicitude throughout the kingdom or empire. But *we are a nation of sovereigns; and our children*, princes of a future generation. Great care should, therefore, be exercised in the selection of teachers for every grade of schools.

And what are some of the

NECESSARY QUALIFICATIONS

of the good teacher? This is a practical question, and one which it seems proper to answer in this connection. In the past, too little attention has been given to this subject. The writer well remembers the time when no examinations were required of candidates for teachers of our common schools: and, in many cases, the only questions raised by the school-officer as to the fitness of the applicant for the important office, were, first, Is he physically strong and courageous? second, Will he work cheap? third, Will he consent to "board round"?

These questions settled affirmatively, the candidate was sure to be employed. False opinions then very generally prevailed. It was believed that good school-government could be maintained only by physical force; and that *anybody* who could read, write, and cipher, and "wield the birch," could keep school. And another serious error *was* and *is* entertained; viz., that a backward school does not need a well-qualified teacher: while the fact is, such a school demands all the more attention because it is backward. From such erroneous views has arisen much of the indifference manifested by parents as to the qualifications of their teachers. Still it is a vital question; and I wish to direct to it, especially, the attention of my readers.

PHYSICAL VIGOR.

Let me say, then, to the school-committees intrusted with the important duty of selecting teachers for their public schools, Inquire, first of all, for physical vigor (not flogging-power, but *health*) in your candidate. No employment taxes more severely the vital energies, or demands more vigorous health, than the successful management and instruction of a school. The teacher's is a *confined* life. He has but few leisure days or hours, and but short vacations, that he can call his own. During six hours every day, for at least five days in a week, he is shut up between four walls, and often in a badly-ventilated and uncomfortable room; and has but little opportunity for the necessary exercise and recreation.

His is also a *laborious* life. If faithful to his charge, his labors are incessant. He must govern and teach, and teach and govern, and sometimes under the most discouraging circumstances. Out of school, his hours are devoted to a preparation for his work, — reading, studying, thinking, planning, for the improvement and welfare of his pupils.

Again: the teacher's life is full of *care* and *anxiety*. He is laden with responsibility which he cannot shift if he would. Not only do his confinement and unremitting toil tax his strength, and wear upon his constitution, but his perplexing cares and anxious watchings shock his nervous system. Toilsome days and anxious nights are a constant strain upon his very life. To endure all this, and sustain himself under so severe a pressure, the teacher must enjoy good health.

Common Sense.

The second requisite qualification for a good teacher is *common sense.* This may seem to some to be superfluous; but not so. There is much more *uncommon* than common sense among men; and yet the latter is indispensable to success in the vocation of teaching. The teacher occupies a very important position. He is thrown upon his own resources; must act every day without aid or counsel upon questions which have an important bearing upon his success or failure. And what shall guide him to the choice of the best means to meet the emergency, and to accomplish his object? He cannot consult his professional books or his more experienced and wise fellow-teachers; but he must act without delay. And what but his common sense can guide him to a judicious course of action? In the management and government of his school, and in all his intercourse with the families of his patrons, he will meet a thousand opportunities to exercise this noble gift, this instinct of nature. Let parents see to it, therefore, that their teachers possess good common sense.

Cheerful and Hopeful Disposition.

Another of Nature's special gifts to the successful teacher of children is *a cheerful and hopeful disposition.*

Some persons are constitutionally gloomy and desponding. They always look on the dark side of this bright world; never see the "silver lining" that gilds the dark cloud overhanging them; and hence they wear upon their countenance, and express in their words, a funereal gloom that dispels all cheerfulness, and shuts out the sunlight from the heart. These men and women despair of the future; anticipate no good for themselves or for others; and hence settle down in gloomy despondency to brood over their misfortunes. Now, it requires no argument to show the undesirableness of placing these desponders in the school-room.

"As the teacher is, so is the school." The gloom and hopelessness which he cherishes will be imparted to his pupils, to suppress their cheerfulness, dampen their enthusiasm, and discourage their efforts. The expression of his countenance, the tones of his voice, and indeed his very presence, cast a gloom over the buoyant hearts of childhood and youth.

On the other hand, the cheerful and hopeful teacher inspires his pupils with his own spirit, and animates them by his own living example. And children need this inspiration and encouragement more than instruction. Their improvement while in school depends upon nothing so much as the happy smile and cheerful words of the hopeful and enthusiastic teacher. This very hopefulness enables the teacher to secure the best results of his well-directed efforts. He has to deal with dulness and stupidity; and he sees little or no improvement from day to day. He is sometimes ready to give up in despair; but he remembers that the development of mind, like the growth of the tree, is by slow and imperceptible degrees. The sturdy oak that now defies the storm and tempest is the product of a hundred years; and the intellect and character which give manhood and womanhood a proud pre-eminence in positions of influence and usefulness have often been unfolded by the patient toil of the hopeful teacher under the most trying difficulties. Let it not be forgotten by parents, therefore, that nothing can compensate for the want of a cheerful and hopeful disposition in the instructors of their children.

Love of Children.

The *love of children* is still another necessary natural qualification of the teacher. Some possess it, and some do not; and when a candidate for the high office of primary teacher especially presents herself, who has not this fondness for children in some degree at least, she should be at once rejected on that account.

This love of children qualifies the teacher to be happy in their presence, to be patient with their childishness, and to sympathize with them in all their enjoyments and trials.

It is interesting to see how children

are drawn, as by magnetism, to the teacher who loves them. They form her acquaintance at sight; believe in her, and cling to her as to their own mother (whose place she occupies, and whose responsibilities she has assumed); and of course they are ready to obey her, and profit by her example, precepts, and instruction. This love of the teacher for her pupils always inspires their love for her in a corresponding degree. They seek her society, and enjoy her presence; they follow her and cling to her as she winds her way over the hill and through the valley to and from the school; they welcome her to their homes, and entertain her by their smiles and childish prattle; they invite her to mingle in their sports; and she becomes a child again while with children. It is not strange, therefore, that mutual sympathy is awakened, and mutual friendship created, such as will give the teacher unbounded control over her pupils in the management and discipline of her school.

Love for the Work.

Nearly allied to the love of children, as a natural and necessary qualification of the true teacher, is *a love for the work.* Fondness for the society of the young tends to make the business of teaching agreeable; but this is not all that is necessary. Such other qualifications are implied as create a taste for the details of the teacher's work, and prepare him to endure patiently the burdens and vexations of school-life. He is patient and persevering, industrious and faithful, because he finds a positive pleasure in the performance of each required duty. He estimates the dignity and responsibility of the teacher's profession from a higher standpoint, and cherishes a proud satisfaction in the nobility of his position and the important results of his labors.

Aptness to Govern and Teach.

Aptness to govern and to teach is still another natural gift to be sought in the candidate for the teacher's office.

Aptness to govern is expressed in the word *authority*, and implies ability to direct and control others. It is inborn, and manifests itself as a kind of *instinct.* It is seen among children when assembled to engage in their sports; perhaps in

> "Some village Hampden, that, with dauntless breast,
> The little tyrant of his fields withstood."

Some one assumes the command, and exercises his gift to rule. It is seen among men. Whenever they organize for any purpose,

> "Some Cromwell, guiltless of his country's blood,"

becomes the leader, and exercises authority and control. In some families the children are in complete subjection to their parents, and yet no special effort has ever been made to govern them. The mother has *authority*, which is discovered in her eye, in the tones of her voice, in her truthful words and unchangeable purposes. Under her management the habit of obedience is soon formed, and cheerful submission rendered.

In some schools (though these are the exception, and not the rule) the master has only to wave his hand, or tap with his pencil upon the desk, to restore perfect order. His very presence is a ruling power, which his pupils are inclined to recognize and obey. He has authority, a natural aptness to govern. Lack of discipline in the family and school, which has become so fearful an evil in our land, more often results from a want of this native power than from any other cause.

Aptness to teach is not always connected with aptness to govern, but is equally desirable as a qualification for the important duties our teachers have to perform. Ability to teach well implies the power to interest and fix the attention of the pupil or class; the power to illustrate and apply principles; the power to read character, so as to be able to adapt instruction to the varying capacities and dispositions of different pupils; and the discretion to know what to teach, when to teach, and how much to teach. Aptness to teach does not necessarily imply the highest order of scholarship, nor the largest ability to understand and explain a given lesson; but the power to inspire, guide, and control pupils in self-culture, and in the attainment of knowledge by their own earnest application.

School-trustees should spare no pains, in the selection of teachers for their schools, to find those who possess these peculiar gifts. And they should examine the candidate also in reference to another qualification; viz., *energy of character*, or what is appropriately called "snap." One *live* teacher is worth a score of *dead* ones. He will accomplish much more work; and his presence and influence are inspiring, not only in the schoolroom, but in the homes of the children and by the way. A live teacher makes a live school, and awakens a new interest in the cause of popular education in the community where he resides. This vital energy of which I speak enlivens his whole being. It is seen in the elasticity of his step, and in his animated conversation. It flashes from his eyes, and streams from his fingers, as the red current of life courses rapidly through his

veins, propelled by a heart, every fibre of which throbs with sympathetic emotion, and a lively interest in the work in which he is engaged. Energy is essential to success in any enterprise, and especially in the difficult and important work of managing and teaching school.

Well-Balanced Mind.

And the teacher of our children should have *a well-balanced and highly-cultivated mind.*

The man or woman of "one idea," the mere visionary of eccentric habits, should never be tolerated in the schoolroom. Such a person has distorted views of life, and false principles of action; and is an unsafe exemplar and guide of youth. The educator, above all men, should have a sound mind, a clear judgment, and a comprehensive knowledge of men and things. All his mental faculties should be fully developed, and in harmonious action; and this implies not only soundness, but culture. And that culture should be *liberal;* by which I mean, the mind should be disciplined by hard study, and stored by extensive information gathered from the broad field of science, history, and literature. It is not enough that our teachers understand merely the branches to be taught in our schools: they should be intellectual *men* and *women*, who have the power of systematic thought; the power to analyze, classify, and reason; and the power to employ their varied culture and attainments in the business and duties of practical life. Such teachers only are well furnished for their work; and such only should be regarded as suitable candidates for the high office which they are called to fill.

I have urged the desirableness of extensive culture for all our teachers. I must now insist upon the necessity of *a thorough knowledge of the primary branches.* This implies, first of all, a knowledge of the principles which underlie the science of arithmetic, geography, grammar, history, &c. These principles, with the reasons and application to the science, must be learned and made familiar, or the teacher has no ability to instruct successfully. It is important, therefore, to inquire how thoroughly the candidate (for whatever grade of school) has been trained in these principles and facts.

NORMAL TRAINING.

But this is not enough. Our teachers must be *professionally trained.* We have given them a position of great dignity; have intrusted them with a work of vast importance; and we require of them duties of fearful import. "To teach," says Dr. Channing, "whether by word or action, is the greatest function on earth;" and can it be that they need no *special* preparation for their work?

We require of our physician, our lawyer, and our clergyman, that he should be professionally educated. It is not enough that he has been thoroughly drilled in academic halls; not enough that he has been liberally educated. We do not intrust to him the life of our child, unless he has studied medicine; nor an important suit in chancery, unless he has studied law; nor do we regard him qualified to preach the gospel, unless he has studied theology.

Yea, more. We require a professional training for the common mechanic, the farmer, the sailor, and indeed for every art, trade, and occupation. We do not allow a man to build a house, to cultivate a farm, to navigate a ship, to shoe a horse, to repair a watch, nor even to shave the hair from the chin, who has not served an apprenticeship in order to learn the special art we expect him to practise.

Now, "teaching is an art, and the teacher an artist," — an art of the greatest difficulty and highest importance. And shall we continue to intrust the business of educating our children to those who have had no opportunity for normal instruction? — to the mere novice, simply because she knows a little of arithmetic, geography, and grammar? Nothing can be more inconsistent and unwise than to assign a work so important to those who have no skill, and who have been untaught in the profession.

We have our schools of law, of medicine, and of divinity. We regard them as a necessity. We require an apprenticeship in every trade, and in every kind of business. This, too, is highly appropriate and necessary to the end in view. We expect none to undertake the duties of these professions or trades who have not had this special preparation. But, until within a few years, no provision was made for the professional training of teachers; nor was it regarded of any importance. The impression prevailed that anybody could keep school; and hence anybody who would serve an ignorant constituency in this *menial* office for a very small compensation was employed. But I trust a brighter day has dawned. Normal schools have, at length, been established in nearly every State in the Union, and a multitude of teachers have been gathered into them. Still, only a small part of the teachers of our public schools have yet been reached. And this is not the worst feature of the case. The majority do not feel its importance. They can secure their certificates, fulfil their engagements, and receive their wages; and hence they are satisfied.

The great responsibility in this matter, after all, rests upon parents. They do not *demand* the professionally-educated teachers. They too often prefer those not qualified, if only they will consent to work for less pay, and submit to more hardships. Let it be understood throughout our country that no candidates for the teacher's office will be accepted unless they are normally educated, as it is understood that no one can practise medicine unless he has studied the "healing art," and soon normal schools would be multiplied, and all filled by earnest students preparing themselves for the important work.

It is the duty of parents, therefore, to demand of their teachers higher qualifications. If not educated at the normal school, they should be professionally educated somewhere and in some way. Then would teaching become a profession in the same sense as law or medicine; and our schools would be elevated to a position which their importance demands, and to a usefulness so much to be desired.

A Noble Manhood.

But the crowning excellence of the well-qualified teacher is *a noble manhood or womanhood.* We desire to make men and women of our children. How can we hope to do this, except through the example, influence, and instruction of true manliness or womanliness at home and in the schoolroom? Instructors should possess such qualities and principles as may be safely copied by their pupils. They should have physical vigor, gracefulness of manners, a highly-cultivated and well-furnished mind, a heart full of noble sentiments and swelling with generous emotions, and a character founded upon Christian principle and above suspicion. These virtues we may hope to see ingrafted upon our children. Sure we may be that all the *vices* of the teacher will be copied by his pupils.

To illustrate, I may recall the story of the *china plate.* A fanciful housewife chanced to find among the waste crockery of her hardware merchant a style and figure of plate which greatly pleased her. This specimen was badly cracked and marred: but it showed an exquisitely fine design; and she at once decided to send the plate to China, to have a set manufactured *exactly like* the pattern. This was her order; and it was executed accordingly. Imagine the mortification of the good lady, on receiving her goods, to find the imitation so perfect, that all the *defects* of the old plate had been wrought into the new!

So parents may expect the reproduction of the teacher in their children, with all the spots and stains which are found upon his character. Let them look well, therefore, to the qualifications of those to whom they intrust so important a charge.

Female Teachers

have taken the field of education as by conquest. More than two-thirds of the public schools of our land are managed and taught by women. A change was produced by the war of the Rebellion, which called into military service a large number of young men who had been employed in teaching. But the reason why women are and will be retained in the schools is found in the fact that they are peculiarly fitted for the business of teaching. Woman is the divinely appointed teacher of her race. She has natural endowments and special fitness for the work in the school as well as in the family. She has proved herself not only "apt to teach," but also capable of managing and governing successfully. Her quick sensibilities, ardent sympathies, natural love for the true, the beautiful, and the good, her patience, perseverance, and enthusiasm, eminently qualify her for this important field of labor. Children are drawn to her as by a natural instinct: they trust in her with implicit confidence.

Hence woman is especially adapted to the primary and intermediate schools. In selecting a teacher, the woman of equal qualifications should always be preferred to the man for either department. She has also honored the profession in important positions in the academy and seminary; and, in some instances, at the head of these institutions.

As a class, woman has a higher standard of morals and manners. She does not "smoke," nor "drink," nor "swear," nor waste her time loafing in places of public resort. And she has more refined feelings and manners; and therefore she has more power to gain the affections and win the confidence of the young who are ready to profit by the influence of her correct habits and good example.

And woman is not only adapted to the care and instruction of children in the family and school, but has the capacity for that broad and thorough culture which is essential to the position she occupies. Both in the academic and normal course of studies, she is quite the equal of her brother. The difficulty has been, she has lacked the opportunity to improve and elevate herself. And to-day there is no one thing more important to the welfare of the rising generation than the liberal education of woman. She must mould the family, and give character to the children and youth as they will be found in the school and as citizens in the State. She is relied upon, and must be, chiefly, to manage and instruct our public schools. This fact is not to be regretted, but should be urged as a new plea for her elevation through culture. The schools will be better taught and better managed under her control just as soon as she is allowed time and opportunity to make the necessary preparation. And one of the most important duties which parents owe to their children, in their relations to the school, is, to provide for the education of these teachers. They should not only seek those to instruct their schools who have the best qualifications, but should provide training-schools of high order, that all may be thoroughly fitted for their work. The elevation of the teacher is the elevation of the school, and the surest way to secure the highest improvement of the children. Parents in every State in the Union, in every county, and in every district, one and all, are therefore especially interested in building up and sustaining the Normal School.

Permanency Desirable.

Still another important suggestion to parents in this connection is the permanency of their teachers. If any are so unfortunate as to select a poor teacher for their school, the quicker she is exchanged, the better for all concerned; but, if efficient and desirable, let her be retained as long as possible. The habit of changing teachers, as practised in many districts, twice or three times every year, is ruinous to the school. What can the teacher, who enters the school for one term only, know of the character and peculiarities of her pupils? What motive can she have to adopt and attempt to carry out a systematic course of instruction, when she knows that her successor will be likely to introduce an entirely different course? What can awaken interest in her pupils, or enthusiasm in herself, when she realizes that her work may be undone as soon as she leaves it? And what can the school do to advantage, when nearly all their time is spent in experimenting upon new theories and methods of instruction?

But, with the permanent teacher, every thing is different. On re-opening her school after a vacation, she is cordially greeted by loving and confiding pupils. She knows every class and every scholar, and understands their peculiarities and their wants. On the day of opening, the school can be completely organized, and in good working order. All enter upon their duties with interest and zeal; and the experience of previous terms in the same position enables the teacher to adapt her instruction to the character and standing of her pupils, and the best results are realized.

So it is in every kind of business, as all understand. No business-firm would, if they could avoid it, allow a quarterly exchange of book-keepers in their mercantile-houses, of agents and overseers in their factories, of financiers in their banks, of masters for their merchantmen, of commanders for their iron-clads, or of engineers for their railroads. Business-men make no such blunders. And yet the changes here indicated would be no more disastrous than frequent changes of teachers. We need, first *efficiency*, and then *permanency*. Failing to abide this principle, at least fifty per cent of the real profit of our schools, for the last fifty years, has been lost.

Public Schools and a Free State.

I have elsewhere argued the importance of the family in its relations to the State; and have urged fidelity in family discipline, that the children may be fitted for the important duties of citizenship. I now come to consider the public school in its relations to our free government.

The character of the school is determined by the character of the families of which it is composed; and the State must become what the family and school have made it.

The American common school, as planted in New England and transplanted in every free State in the Union, is, in an important sense, a political institution, and the very corner-stone of our government. It is not a purely scholastic, domestic, nor ecclesiastic institution; and yet it has a close connection with the university, the family, and the church. In it the American people have their first drill in public life. The child who enters the public schoolroom for the first time knows public life; and there can be no substitute for the peculiar education in citizenship he there receives. A public school in America is a little republic, where children of all orders of society, and every grade of culture, are taught to live together under a common system of law, governed by public officials whose authority is backed by the whole power of the State. There, during the period of school-life, he rehearses every phase of the public life of his country. There he receives that mental illumination and rudimentary knowledge which help him to be an intelligent citizen. There he gains the more important instruction in personal character as related to others living under law. There he learns how to conduct himself in his relations to his fellow-men, and to respect their rights.

When we consider the exclusiveness of family-life, the clannish tendency of all business-connections, the violent prejudices that influence individual members of homes, churches, and professional cliques, we can realize the importance of that generous discipline of manhood and womanhood which alone can fit our children for American citizenship. The public school only can instruct the masses of American people in what pertains to public character and public virtue. It stands next above the family; and is the first step out of that divine institution into that other divine organization, the State. And, if we can determine what is the most essential element of our national prosperity, we shall understand what is the most important lesson to be taught in our public schools. And can any doubt that that element is public virtue, and that lesson the morality of the Bible? There was no question, among our wise, practical, and devout ancestors who established the American public school, about its right and imperative duty to teach morality, and so much of religious truth as is essential to it. Indeed, the original common school of our free States was a seminary of earnest moral patriotism. Moral instruction bore a large proportion to the entire work of the school. The Bible was the reading-book. The master who failed to maintain a high standard of character, and who could not preserve order, was turned out. The sermons, exhortations, and prayers in the schoolroom were often more effective for the youthful congregation than those emanating from the pulpit. This emphasis on moral and patriotic culture in the old schoolhouse was one of the most powerful elements of our national success.

The common school of our day has made great progress in the line of outward accommodations, and methods of scientific and literary instruction; but we may fear that it is losing its original power as the national teacher of public character. As a scientific agency, it has been prodigiously enlarged; but it is in danger of losing that which once made it our national sheet-anchor, as the natural teacher of public virtue, and the training-school of American citizenship. Intellectual brilliancy is too often, under the name of "culture," allowed to override every thing. Instruction in morals and patriotism are too much neglected.

Our government is founded upon the principles of Christianity; and hence the Bible, which is our text-book of Christian morals, should not only be retained, but faithfully taught in our schools, not to impart dogmas and creeds, but to impress its own purifying and life-giving precepts upon the tender heart of childhood. The personal and religious character of our teachers should be a matter of earnest solicitude and inquiry on the part of those who are intrusted with the guardianship of public instruction.

The people's school should be cherished as a national birthright: it should be located upon every hill-top and in every valley, throughout the length and breadth of this vast country; it should receive the fostering care of our state and central governments; it should bring within its enclosure, for culture and instruction, all children of school-age, and of every sect and condition in life; for all are to become citizens, to share the responsibility and to enjoy the blessings of our free institutions.

Every effort of mistaken or misguided men to subvert the public school, to change its character and office, and to turn it to secular and partisan purposes, should be firmly and earnestly resisted. Our laws guarantee to all religious freedom. Every man, and class of men, are protected in the enjoyment of their own religious views, and modes of worship. Hence it is not proper that the public school, established for the education of the whole people, should be under ecclesiastical and partisan control.

Now, if we would cherish and sustain our free government, and preserve untarnished for coming generations the blessings which it is calculated to bestow, we must turn back to the common school bequeathed us by our fathers, which took under its guardianship the public morals, and inculcated the pure principles of patriotism. We must cling to the Bible, the true source of all moral instruction, and insist upon instilling its conservative and purifying principles into the minds and hearts of our children, and ingrafting them into their lives. The present form of government in America is the logical growth of a Christian civilization which would be impossible without the Christian morality found in the New Testament. All our great political conflicts are essentially moral; and we must realize the truth, that we have no security in the present or the future, except in the faithful training of our children, in the family and the school, according to the genius and spirit of our peculiar institutions. To cast off this duty of the State to teach public virtue and Christian patriotism in her schools would be a criminal surrender of important principles and our dearest rights, and would result in nothing less than political suicide.

Compulsory Attendance.

Our children belong to the State. They will become citizens of this great republic: and if it is true, as I have asserted, that the public school alone can instruct them in what pertains to public character and public virtue; if here alone we can hope to give them that culture and intelligence which are necessary to American citizenship, — it must follow that the common school is a necessity, and that its object will not be accomplished until all the children in the nation shall enjoy its advantages.

Just here comes in the plea for *compulsory* education.

The necessity for universal intelligence and virtue to the perpetuity of a free government was understood and provided for by our Pilgrim ancestors. Their first and greatest efforts were made in this direction. They established the public school for the very purpose of imparting to the masses gratuitous primary instruction and the morality of the Bible; but they failed to see the importance of making attendance upon these schools obligatory. Hence thousands upon thousands of unthinking or ungrateful parents in every free State in the Union have allowed their children to grow up in ignorance and vice, to their own injury and the peril of the republic. Conscious of this mistake, and of the alarming evils resulting from it, several of our States have already added a compulsory clause to their school-laws; and when the whole American people shall have reached the same conclusion, and a *general* law compelling school-attendance shall have been enacted, the task of government will be much easier, and the results flowing from popular rule will be much more hopeful as the moral tone of the nation is elevated.

United Germany and Switzerland owe their greatest strength and security to that feature of their laws which compels parents to educate their children; and such a law is equally consistent with the genius of our own government.

Our school-system was established, and has been maintained, under the superintendence of State authority. We compel our citizens to pay school-taxes, to build and furnish schoolhouses, employ teachers, and procure books; and may we not with as much reason compel them to allow their children to avail themselves of the advantages thus provided? The public weal demands the school as a means of safety; and, to the same end, it demands *attendance* upon this school. A free State has a right to maintain its own freedom by compulsory laws; and hence it has the right, and it is its duty, to compel intelligence in every instance where ignorance would be the result of voluntary action.

And the propriety of compulsory laws in a republican form of government may be seen by still further examples, drawn from our own statute-books. The preservation of the State requires a military force which the executive may raise and control at discretion. The army and navy are necessary to repel invasion, and subdue rebellion; and we find provision made in our laws for either emergency. We not only have a standing army and navy subject to the absolute control of our President, but a militia composed of our able-bodied citizens, who are subject to a *compulsory* draft for military service. But is it consistent with personal freedom under a free government to compel a citizen to leave his home, his family, and his business, to enter upon the hard and dangerous service of the camp and the battle-field for the good of his country, and not consistent to compel him to educate his children in the free public schools to the same end?

May we compel a child to enter the State Reform School, or House of Correction, and not rightfully compel him to attend the public school, which may prevent the crime he has committed? May we inflict severe penalties upon those who have outraged the community by their crimes, and not be allowed to enforce the education of that class of children and youth from which nine-tenths of all our criminals come?

Every law is an infringement upon the personal freedom of that citizen who is disposed to violate it; but such personal liberty must be restrained, and such laws must be enforced as have in view the good of the State.

Our free government is based upon the principle of freedom under law. It guarantees the right of every citizen to do as he pleases, so long as he pleases to do right. It restrains him from doing what is wrong, so far as that wrong inflicts an injury upon the State. Judged by this principle, no man has any right to allow his children to grow up in idleness, ignorance, and vice. The State has provided the opportunity for their free education; and, if they do not improve it, they become a source of social danger. Idleness and ignorance are sure conditions of vice and crime; and these are elements of national decay.

It becomes the imperative duty of parents, therefore, not only to provide the best advantages for the education of their children in free public schools, but also to see to it that such a law is enacted and enforced as will insure the education of every man's children in the neighborhood and State.

Parents' Relations to Teachers.

Parents have special duties to perform in the relations they sustain to their teachers. If well qualified and faithful, as we demand, these teachers have a right to claim fidelity and co-operation on the part of their employers.

They should receive fair compensation for their valuable services.

I see no reason why teaching should not be as remunerative as other professional labor, which is estimated not only as service, but in view of the time and money spent in preparation. It is an admitted principle, that wages should be increased in proportion to the knowledge and skill attained in every department of industry.

Common physical labor has its value; and the same labor, when directed by that intelligence and special ability which qualify for leadership, as master-workmen, may demand more compensation. And if the preparation for the desired service requires special training; if years of time and much money are necessary to make that service available, as in the learned professions, — salaries are raised accordingly.

Hence the superintendent may receive much more than the common operative; the physician may demand as much for a single visit as his patient would receive for a day's labor; and the lawyer for an hour's pleading, as much as his client for a month's service.

It must follow, therefore, that the well-qualified teacher should receive more pay than the common day-laborer or the illiterate household drudge. And yet, in times past, this principle has not been recognized; and our public school-teachers have been so poorly paid, that the better class have, in many instances, sought other and more lucrative employments. It is hoped that wiser counsels will prevail, and that parents everywhere will see not only the propriety, but the necessity, of employing the best teachers at their command, and paying them liberally for their services.

And teachers should have provided for them a permanent and pleasant home in the district where they teach.

I will not deny that there are some advantages in the old practice of boarding the schoolmaster "around."* He is thus compelled to form an intimate acquaintance with his patrons, and to learn the peculiarities and wants of each family. He may thus gain influence and power in the management of his school by securing the confidence and co-operation of his pupils and their parents. Still all these social advantages can be gained, without the evil contemplated, by visiting these families at their homes, as the teacher should always do.

No one more needs the conveniences and comforts of a home than the laborious and care-worn instructress of our children. She needs it for rest and comfort while she can be released from the excitement and toil of the schoolroom.

* The author is aware that the habit of boarding the teacher round is much less common than years ago. Still it prevails in the rural districts to some extent, and hence should receive a passing notice in this connection.

She needs it that she may have time and opportunity to prepare herself for her important school-duties. And she needs it in common with all other civilized human beings; as "there is no place like home," even though it be substituted and temporary.

What should we think of the church that should require their pastor to board among his parishioners; that should compel him to feel that he has among his people "no abiding-place," but must go with his wife and children from house to house to get his daily bread? How much time would such a minister have to prepare himself for his pulpit-services? Indeed, how greatly would his usefulness be abridged by such a foolish effort on the part of his parish to economize!

And suppose the village doctor was required to board among his patients? Such an idea would be ridiculed as preposterous; but why more unreasonable to require the minister and doctor to board in twenty different families every three months than to require the school-master and school-mistress to do the same?

The teacher needs a steady, pleasant home; and it is not only the imperative duty but the best policy of trustees to provide such a home.

Again: every teacher should be allowed to manage his own school. If not competent to do so, he should not have been employed. If a mistake has been made, and an incompetent person engaged, the difficulty will not be removed by the interference of parents.

Teachers often seek advice, and may profit by it; but any effort on the part of parents to dictate and control in the matter of school-management is not only unwise, but ruinous. The teacher too often finds among his patrons those who presume to give gratuitous information and counsel. Mrs. A., in a very friendly spirit, informs him that her neighbor has some very bad boys who always make trouble in school, and warns him to be on his guard. Mrs. C. thinks it important that he should know how sensitive the parents in that district are on the subject of corporal punishment, and advises him to govern mainly by moral suasion. She assures him, if he will do so, he will be popular and successful.

Mrs. L., an old school-teacher, has, in her own estimation, some excellent ideas upon different methods of instruction; and she is very anxious that the master should adopt them in that school. So the meddlesome mischief-making goes on, until the young teacher is distracted and perplexed beyond measure; and as he cannot, if he would, listen to the suggestions nor follow the advice of all, he is sure to become the subject of tea-party gossip, and of village criticism and abuse, such as will greatly interfere with his usefulness, if it does not prevent his success, in that district.

Wise teachers pay no attention to such unwarrantable interference; and wise parents allow and encourage the teacher to manage his own school in his own way.

Another important idea: Parents should always sustain the teacher in maintaining his authority in the school. That authority is supreme, and may never be trifled with by the pupil.

Unconditional obedience in the school, as well as in the family, is the rule; and the teacher has a right to expect the cordial support of all his patrons in enforcing that rule. The best good of the child, as well as the success of the school, depends upon this co-operation.

Parents are too often ready to listen to the complaints of their children, and to sympathize with them in rebellion against the authority of the school. It would be better never to allow such fault-finding; never to criticise, but always to sustain the teacher in the presence of children. If they can have the encouragement of parents in their recklessness at school, they will become bold and defiant, and will paralyze, if they do not destroy, the influence and efforts even of the best teachers.

But grant that the teacher is in fault; that he is really inefficient, and the school comparatively worthless: it is better to sustain even a poor teacher for months than to allow the pupils to have any agency in breaking up the school. If an incompetent teacher is to be dismissed, it should be done by the independent action of the *district*, and not at the suggestion or by the aid of pupils in rebellion. Let

them be kept in subjection by whatever means necessary, without regard to the efficiency or inefficiency of the government in power. Obedience and fidelity are required of them in all their relations to the school, no matter under what circumstances they are placed. If all parents should take this view of the subject, and so co-operate and sustain their teachers, our public schools would be vastly more efficient and useful than they ever have been; the spirit of insubordination which has manifested itself to an alarming extent within a few years past, in our public schools, academies, and colleges, would soon be crushed out; and our children, as they come up to assume the responsibilities of life, would become obedient and loyal citizens, and faithful subjects under the government of God. We little realize how much the discipline of the family and the school have to do

in forming the character and habits of the future man and woman as they will appear in their relations to the State and under the divine law. Mothers and teachers, under God, make them what they are, and through them determine the character and destiny of the nation.

Again: parents should encourage their teacher by manifesting a real interest in his work, and by a hearty co-operation in all his efforts to benefit the school. Such sympathy and aid have their influence, not only upon the teacher, but upon the school. Children are creatures of impulse. They are greatly influenced by circumstances, and in school-matters by nothing more than by the interest or apathy manifested by their parents.

It must follow, therefore, that if parents would see their schools prosper, and their children rising from grade to grade in a thorough and systematic course of study, they must manifest a deep interest and an earnest enthusiasm in every thing that pertains to the school.

They do not expect success in any other enterprise without oversight and interest. The tea-party, the sewing-circle, the missionary-association, which are organized in every community for social and benevolent purposes, could not prosper without the earnest attention of the mothers and matrons who are interested in them. No farmer would intrust the training of his animals to exhibit at a county-fair or upon the race-ground without a personal supervision, and a deep interest manifested in every stage of progress. The servants who have the direct care of these animals are encouraged by words of approval and praise, and an abiding sympathy in all the details of the process. And can it be a matter of less importance and of less interest to parents that their own children are under the process of training for the stage of life and for immortality? and can they afford to give up this work of education so entirely to others, that both the teacher and the children lose the inspiring influence of an approving smile and an encouraging word from them as they toil on in their arduous work?

Next come the specific duties which parents have to perform in these relations. The degree of interest which they feel in the working of their school is manifest,—

1. In their efforts to secure constancy and punctuality of attendance. Every intelligent parent understands the importance of this suggestion. Children who do not give their undivided time and attention to the school suffer an irreparable loss of time, of ability, and of interest. The days, half-days and hours of absence

and tardiness frequently amount to weeks in terms, and months in years. And this is not all: the loss of ability to study successfully results from the loss of time. Lessons are dependent upon each other; and when one is learned, and the next omitted, the scholar has no ability to understand the third: he acquires superficial habits of study, becomes discouraged, and loses his interest in his lessons and in the school. And still further: the class and the school to which he belongs suffer in consequence of his absences. The teacher's time is taxed in giving him extra instruction; and yet he drags behind his class. And thus, not unfrequently, scholars of good ability accomplish nothing, and lose all the benefit of the school, in consequence of tardiness and frequent absences which it is the duty of parents to prevent. And, beyond all these evil results, the habit of irregularity is formed, which follows the child through life. He who is habitually tardy at school will be tardy at church, tardy in business, and unreliable everywhere.

And it is equally objectionable to allow children leave of absence before the regular hour for dismission. Parents should so arrange their business and their meals as to give their children the full control of their time during the term of school; and then they should insist upon constant and punctual attendance. A word to the wise is sufficient on this point.

2. The interest parents feel in the success of their school appears also in their efforts to encourage fidelity and studiousness in their children.

Parents should not only give their children the time while the school is in session, and insist upon their constancy and punctuality in attendance, but should also impress upon them the importance of improving the opportunities thus afforded. Much may be done to aid in the successful working of the school by earnest home-counsel. Point out to these children the personal advantages to be realized in the future by those who improve their youth by self-culture. Show them that their relative position in society, their influence and usefulness, depend upon the manner in which they spend their fleeting school-days. Encourage them faithfully to prepare every lesson assigned them, and to cherish a deep interest in every school-exercise, as a means to the end in view.

Who can fail to see, that, if such an interest should be manifested and such an influence exerted in every family in the district by the parents, a power would be brought to bear upon the school which would be felt for good in its elevation and prosperity? Teachers would by such co-operation be inspired with new hope and encouragement, and would renew their diligence and fidelity in the noble work in which they are engaged. A want of such encouragement and aid has been a fruitful source of difficulty and failure in the public schools of our country.

3. Parents who have a suitable degree of interest will seek frequent opportunities to visit their schools.

Every parent in every district in the nation should visit his children's school at least twice during every term. These visits should not be made for the purpose of interfering with the discipline of the school, or of assisting in conducting its exercises. It is presumed that the teacher employed is entirely competent to manage his own affairs. But parents should visit their schools to learn how they are conducted, and to manifest their interest in the education of their children. These occasional visits will do more than any thing else can do to rouse and encourage the teacher, and to inspire the pupils with zeal and earnestness in the discharge of their school-duties. Such visits have a decided influence over the deportment of the school. They tend to cultivate pride of character, school-pride, and self-respect in the pupils, and to check all tendencies to disorder and rebellion. Few children are so abandoned and reckless as to indulge in improper conduct in the presence of visitors, or so lost to self-respect as to feel no interest in the reputation of the school. Hence under such restraint they learn to cultivate the habit of good order, and to give respectful attention.

Again: parental visits have an influence to secure a higher order of scholarship in the school. They awaken a new interest, and create a new zeal, in the work of the schoolroom. Children have a laudable desire to appear well in the presence of critics; and hence they will labor to prepare their lessons.

These are some of the obvious and necessary results of a faithful discharge of parental duty in school relations.

And it seems proper here to inquire of parents, as a practical question, how far they have performed these duties.

Have *you*, my friend, whose eye may fall upon this printed page, always sustained the teacher of your children in maintaining the authority of the school? Have you encouraged that teacher by your own manifest zeal, interest, and co-operation in the arduous and important work you have assigned him? And, to be more specific, have you made special efforts to secure the constant and punc-

20*

tual attendance of your children upon the exercises of the school? Have you encouraged their fidelity and studiousness as pupils by earnest and constant appeals to their reason and conscience?

.And, finally, do you visit your school at frequent intervals, and thus inspire and encourage your children and their teacher in the noble work you have given them to do? If so, do it more faithfully hereafter: if not, from this hour wake up to a consciousness of your obligations in this regard, and henceforth do your duty.

X.

THE CHILDREN IN SOCIETY.

DURING all these years of home and school life, our children must mingle more or less in society. Hence, in the discipline of the family, parental watchfulness and care must have regard also to this source of educational influence and danger.

Childhood is confined, for the most part, to the family-circle. Its associations are formed amid the endearing relations of home. Away from the strife and bustle of the world, it breathes a purer atmosphere, and feels the more exalted and refining influences of love and affection.

Youth is more exposed. It mingles in the village and the school with companions and strangers, and necessarily receives the impress of their example. The daily transactions of life, the public meeting, the customs, manners, and laws of society, the arts, the professions, — all these, which constitute the real life of manhood, bring a powerful influence to bear upon our children long before they reach maturity.

And, that we may understand how far parental responsibility extends in this direction, let us inquire to what extent the influence of society may control the education and determine the destiny of these children. This influence, as brought to bear upon them for good or for evil, may be regarded as threefold; viz., the positively bad, the negatively bad, and the positively good.

The positively bad influence is found

in the prevalence in community of false views of life, erroneous principles, and a corrupt state of public taste and morals. The influence of the wretched habits of thought, feeling, and action, that is often found in community, is sufficient to counteract, neutralize, or destroy the results of the most successful education. And this controlling influence of society is felt much earlier than is generally supposed. Could the mother's love and pure example control the child until early manhood, he would be comparatively safe; but how often is public example responsible for impressions made upon the almost infant spirit! — for a train of influences which contaminate the atmosphere of the nursery and the schoolroom! How often has the true mother, acting in all the dignity of her exalted position, by a calm and Christian spirit and a pure Christian example, instructed, refined, and elevated her child, until, under God, it seemed to be allied to the angels in its nature! — and still as often the world has come in to mar her beautiful workmanship, and sometimes to destroy it.

It follows, therefore, that either these corrupting influences of society must be removed, or counteracted and controlled by the special vigilance and earnest action of parents in the training of their children.

And the negatively bad influence of society produces much evil to the cause of education. The child comes from the bosom of the family, his heart all glowing with the kindly influences of home, and a love of the pure and beautiful: the pupil leaves the school, where he has tasted the sweets of learning, and felt the inspiring influence of the earnest and true teacher's example. They enter the community where there is felt but little interest for the child, or his school, or his education. Their warm affections meet a cold and lifeless formality. Their thoughts are diverted from the themes connected with their own culture and elevation to the world of fashion, politics, and speculation. And what must be the influence of such a change upon the child and the pupil? It cannot fail to paralyze or destroy every effort for his improvement, and all the beneficial results of any nominal system of education.

A positively good educational influence in society implies the existence of a high tone of moral and religious sentiment, a deep and abiding interest in the education of the children at home and in school, and a corresponding activity both in private and public. More than half a century ago, Edmund Burke, in speaking of the English and French nobility, said the French had the advantage of the English in being surrounded by a powerful out-guard of military education. How powerful that out-guard was against the attack of an internal foe, the strange history of that nation will show.

How much more wise and noble the purpose of society to protect the rising generation by implanting around them the more powerful out-guard of a thorough *Christian* education! The educational influence of society thus constituted would be great beyond comparison. It would not only protect the tender interests of those well educated in the family, but would gather in the neglected and half-ruined from the "hedges" and "highways," and train *them* also for usefulness. Society should be itself a school, capable of imparting every lesson and precept fitted to elevate and enrich the human character. It should be the guardian of domestic and public education, of private and public virtue, and the exemplar of that religion which purifies the heart and elevates the affections.

The historian informs us that the laws of Lycurgus and Solon were only the public sentiment of the age in which they lived, and that their names have been immortalized for doing what circumstances demanded. Fortunate it would be if such a state of public sentiment existed among us as would not only create wholesome laws, but the necessity of their execution; as would not only compel us to feel the importance of education to our individual, social, and civil welfare, but to act consistently with such a conviction. The cause of popular education in our country needs the genuine protection, and true-hearted, life-inspiring sympathy, of the public.

SPECIAL DANGERS.

The special dangers to which our children are exposed, as they come out of the family to mingle in society, may now be considered.

And, first, I will name *corrupt associations.* Where is the city, the village, or neighborhood, in which may not be found the dissipated, profane, and vile? And how often do they disturb the public peace by boisterous demonstrations, consume the products of industry by their idleness and waste, sap the foundations of virtue, and pollute the very atmosphere they breathe!

In large cities these corrupters of youth sometimes organize in order to practise their iniquity with more success. They follow gambling, thieving, robbery, and murder, as a business, and extend their operations far and near in every direction. Their representatives, more or less mature in the art of crime, are scattered over the rural districts. Everywhere they exert their pernicious influence over the unwary and artless youth by whom they are surrounded; and these, too, become contaminated.

In the beginning, it is not so much the fault as the misfortune of these victims of dissipation and crime that they fall into this evil way. In many instances, the most noble traits of character are the source of their greatest danger. They are genial, generous, and confiding, and hence companionable and sympathetic, and ready to follow where others may lead. They do not suspect the evil to which they are exposed, nor the pitfalls which lie along the path they tread; and hence the danger is all the more alarming.

Corrupt associations are at first more

commonly met in the streets, in loafers' hall, and in the bar-room, where the idle and vicious are accustomed to congregate. Once initiated, these impulsive youth are led along by a natural process, and by slow degrees are hardened for the crimes of maturer life. They may find their way to the house of correction, the reform-school, or the prison; or they may escape these reforming agencies, and become desperate characters.

It is sad to remember that these corrupting influences are sometimes met by children of tender age in their own homes. The example of a profane, dissipated, and ungodly life is constantly before them. They feel its power, and are drawn by it thus early into the fearful current that nears the whirlpool, and bears its unsuspecting victims towards the threatened ruin. The corrupt society of the school and neighborhood increases the peril in such cases, and makes more sure the destruction that awaits these unfortunate children. If the home-influences have been good, the perils which beset the path of inexperienced youth as they come out to mingle in society is still fearful.

Another source of special danger to the young as they come in contact with the world is a *corrupt literature.*

As soon as our children learn to read, they are exposed to the corrupting influence of the vile trash bearing the name of *literature* with which our country is flooded. It is found in the form of obscene books, periodicals, and papers, which, though strictly prohibited by law from circulating through the mail, find a ready market and an extensive sale. It is found in the illustrated "Police Record" and other sensational works, which tend to excite the vicious propensities, and lead to crime. It is found in the story-telling monthlies and weeklies which are sold by thousands in the streets, at the railroad-stations, on every train of cars, on every line of steamboats, and everywhere that the vender can find a purchaser. The larger proportion of the exciting stories of the present day are strongly impregnated with moral poison, and are fearfully productive of evil to the young.

The several classes of literature to which I have alluded must be regarded as of a decidedly immoral tendency. Our children who come in contact with it cannot shun pollution.

And the whole class of light, cheap literature, as it is written, and read by the multitude, is destructive of the best interests of our children.

Some works of fiction are approved, and may be read with interest and profit;

but *promiscuous* novel-reading, even where there is no *immoral* tendency, serves to weaken the intellect, pervert the taste, and destroy the power of close application which is indispensable to thorough mental discipline and sound scholarship.

"Life is real; life is earnest;" and preparation for its stern duties can never be made by those who waste their time in idle dreaming over the senseless novel of the hour.

And the young are also exposed to the prevalence in community of *perverted views of life, and false views of religious truth.*

And what are the chief aims of men and women in the world, as viewed from the standpoint of pure and artless childhood? Many, it is believed, are actuated by exalted motives to the attainment of noble ends. Such examples stand out in bold relief to adorn the pages of the world's history, and reflect honor upon the race. But how many are seen in the eager pursuit of wealth as the grand object of life! — not as a means of usefulness, but to hoard or squander for their own gratification. And such men are sometimes unscrupulous as to the means by which they aim to gain their object. Few indeed reach by such means the fancied prize, or realize the desired satisfaction; and yet they afford an example of false views of life. Others seek position and power; and how often do they sacrifice their peace, their manliness, their all, for the bubble fame!

Still others bow down and worship at the shrine of fashion and folly. How numerous, how devout, and how servile, this class of worshippers! But is the grand aim of life either the pursuit of wealth, power, or pleasure? Surely there must be a higher and nobler purpose to be attained. But how are our children to view the subject, if taught only by the example of the society in which they mingle? Will they not be likely to adopt the same views of life, and to seek the same selfish end? What shall hinder?

And peril from false views of religious truth is equally alarming. The chilling influence of infidelity on the one hand, and the withering power of fanaticism on the other, will be felt upon them as soon as they leave the protection of the Christian home and school, and even while under parental guardianship. They cannot escape these influences; and the earnest inquiry of every parent should be, how his children may be protected from the evils of society here contemplated.

THE PRACTICAL QUESTION

returns to us, How shall parents protect their children from the public perils which surround them?

In answering this inquiry, I may first suggest, in general, We must rely mainly upon the pleasant home and faithful home-training. To save our children from the corrupting influences of bad associates, they must be separated from them as much as possible. To this end, let home be made pleasant and attractive. Throw around it every charm, and open within it the sources of every rational enjoyment.

Children must be amused; and, if they do not find such amusements at home as their natures crave, they will seek them abroad amid corrupting public influences.

There are sports and games which are harmless in the family-circle, that would lead to dissipation and crime if indulged in the little club-houses and saloons where the reckless and profane are accustomed to congregate; and the practical question for parents to settle is, whether they will provide these means of home-enjoyment for their children, or leave them to spend their long evenings and "rainy days" away from home-protection, and with companions of doubtful character. No sensible parent, it seems to me, can long hesitate on a question so plain. It is idle to talk of holding and restraining these children by the force of authority alone in such matters. It is wise to interest them at home, and thus protect them from the contagion of immoral associations.

To the same end, parents should encourage and patronize such public entertainments as are harmless and profitable, that their children may be occupied, and protected from the exciting and dissipating influences of such exhibitions as are given by "Jim Crow and Company" and kindred troupes through the length and breadth of our land. They pervert the public taste and poison the morals of every community, and cannot fail to reach our youth whose time and attention are not better occupied.

Social neighborhood-gatherings for the young and the old, with their sports and games; the lyceum, with its debating-club and public literary and scientific lectures, — are among the best substitutes for the demoralizing attractions of the outside world.

And how shall our children be protected from the fearful influence of a corrupt literature? It is of the first importance to cultivate in them a taste for the solid branches and hard study. In this way the ground will be pre-occupied. The student whose time is earnestly devoted to the study of language, mathematics, and the sciences, will also be interested in history and the standard works of English literature. He will have no taste for the dissipating and corrupting novel which is thrown in his way. It is the idle brain that craves the excitement of fiction; it is the unoccupied and undisciplined mind that murders time in poring over senseless stories. If the taste is not perverted, the time of our children will be fully employed in profitable study and reading. Correct habits of thought and action will grow with their growth, and strengthen with their strength, until they are fortified against the influences of a perverted literature.

For the same purpose, parents should organize to establish town and village libraries, which should be selected with

the greatest care, for the free use of every family. These should contain books of reference, history, biography, science, and literature; books of criticism, travels, and reviews. From them should be excluded all merely sensational and immoral works of fiction. Such libraries are useful, not only to occupy the time that would otherwise be worse than wasted by many, but they furnish substantial aids to self-culture and improvement.

Great care must also be exercised in selecting magazine and newspaper reading. Among these the serpent is more often coiled, and through them his poison is diffused. Parents should scrupulously exclude from their homes and their public reading-rooms all this spurious and corrupting literature, whether found in the *monthly*, *weekly*, or *daily*.

Their children will then avoid the

temptation and the danger, and will be left to feed upon more healthy diet, and to breathe a purer atmosphere.

With these precautions and safeguards thrown about them, they will be comparatively safe. But the great importance of moral and religious culture, to prepare them to escape the dangerous influences of society, cannot be overestimated.

The chief point to be gained in the discipline of the family is the formation of character. But character must be built upon principle; and principle must draw its vitalizing power from the pure morality of the gospel. External circumstances are important; but internal motives control the will, and regulate the life. Hence our children, to be safe in the midst of public perils, must be "pure in heart," and fully established in the habits of right thought and action.

Human life is a battle-field, in which every youth finds himself opposed by hostile enemies who seek his destruction. Without strength or experience, he is unequal to the contest. He must first be guarded and sustained by the vigilance, wisdom, and strength of those whom God has placed over him. Parental discipline must create and develop self-reliance, and direct self-culture. Surrounded by every means of protection, he must be taught to fight his own battles, and gain his own victories, even to the attainment of a noble character and a pure life.

So may our children withstand the corrupting and insnaring influences of society if they are armed with "the breastplate of righteousness," "the shield of faith," "the helmet of salvation," and "the sword of the Spirit, which is the word of God."

XI.

MISCELLANEOUS SUGGESTIONS.

I TAKE it for granted that parents who read these pages feel the greatest interest in the *results* of family discipline, as applied to their own children, to say the least. Indeed, who can contemplate these results without the deepest solicitude? And if this feeling is cherished from the beginning, and constantly during the whole process of training until the period of maturity is reached, it will tend greatly to secure the end in view.

I have pointed out the danger of mismanagement, and the true system of government in the family. I have attempted to make clear the duties of parents in relation to their schools, the system to be adopted, the outfit to be made, the laws to be enacted and enforced, the necessary qualifications of teachers, and the sympathy and co-operation which they have a right to expect and claim from their employers in their difficult and important work.

But I have not spoken particularly of the erroneous views so prevalent in every community as to the nature and object of a thorough, practical education. I may, therefore, here suggest, with a view to correct, some of these false theories.

By many, education is regarded as valuable only so far as it imparts certain *mechanical accomplishments.* If a child can read and write and cipher, so as to be able to transact the ordinary business of life, some parents think that the end of the school is attained. Others would add certain higher scholastic attainments, such as drawing, painting, music, and a smattering of two or three modern languages, that their children may be liberally educated. Such branches as these they suppose to be all that are necessary for a practical and finished education. They seem to forget that the child has powers and sentiments, which, if uncultivated in early life, will be stifled or perverted so as to become useless or mischievous in riper years; that his moral and intellectual character must be formed, and fixed habits of thought and action established. Whatever the *man* should be, or should do, must result from the training of the *boy*.

These mechanical accomplishments are proper and desirable in their place and time, but do not constitute a practical education.

Another prevailing error, nearly related to the one just noticed, makes education to consist in *acquiring knowledge.*

It is true that knowledge, as attained in the process of education, is a disciplinary agency, and is indispensable to the end in view. But it must not be mistaken for education itself. That consists in the development of power, and not in the attainment of knowledge. The popular error which I here expose assumes that no study is practical which cannot at once be used. Hence, when a solid course of disciplinary studies is recommended, the multitude cry out with Falstaff of honor, —

> "Can honor set to a leg? No: . . . therefore I'll none of it."

With this false notion, the study of the higher mathematics and languages is of no consequence to those who are to be engaged in the common avocations of life. They need only a little *knowledge* of arithmetic, grammar, and history, and perhaps, in some instances, a few facts in natural science.

The same delusion has flooded our country with professional schools (so called) for *mere* boys, who have had no time nor opportunity for the culture necessary to fit them for a course of public instruction. Hence they are rushed through to graduation in the shortest possible course. The beardless boy, who has attended one of our commercial colleges for four short months, comes home with his diploma, and is supposed by his deluded father to have become a full-grown man. He has gained some knowledge, it is claimed, of practical business, and hence is educated. And why do the learned professions turn out so many quacks and pettifoggers, if not from the mistaken notion that education is the attainment of knowledge merely, and is designed to fit the person for some special business or profession?

Under the influence of this same false system, "Science even has turned quack to suit the impatience and impertinence of a money-loving and labor-saving age; and, extracting the quintessence of all subjects, she has put up morals, physics, politics, literature, yea, all things, in convenient and portable forms, and labelled with suitable directions; so that the mere child, by swallowing the diluted and filtered condensation, shall, in an incredibly short time, know more than his grandmother."

And, from this same soil of perverted public opinion, there has sprung up a new crop of school-books and school-systems adapted to this *practical* age. The old subjects are made new and attractive; difficult principles are simplified; hard examples are solved; and the highway to learning, which used to be up the "hill of Science," is now not only a level road, but the journey may be taken at our leisure in saloon-cars. Indeed, under this new system, it is much easier to be educated than to live in ignorance.

This happy era in the book-world is graphically described by one writer in the following language: "The same book-stuff is hashed and cooked in a dozen different ways: pictures now at the top of the page, and questions at the bottom; then pictures and questions reversed; then pictures in the middle, surrounded by a frame of crabbed-looking questions in small type. Wonderful variety! It furnishes big and little potatoes to-day, and little and big potatoes to-morrow."

The end of education is the power or

art of *thinking*. This power is acquired, but never inborn. It is always the price of long-continued and patient study. Talents, though "angel bright," and even genius, need culture, to be educated, as really as the most ordinary intellects. The mere absorption of knowledge, as the sponge absorbs water, gives no discipline; and hence the acquiring of knowledge is not the object to be gained, but the development of mental power.

The educated man has gained the ability to control the exercises of his own mind, to think upon a given subject earnestly and logically, and to reason and judge accurately and correctly. The uneducated man has no such ability: his thoughts are isolated and confused, and his knowledge comparatively useless.

How, then, shall the child be educated? There is but one method. His powers of body, mind, and soul, are to be cultivated and moulded into harmonious manhood through *exercise.* The growth and health of the body depend upon this law. The blacksmith's right arm is made strong and vigorous by constant pounding: the skilful gymnast and the veteran soldier have developed and strengthened their muscular systems by gymnastic and military drill: the musician learns to discourse sweet music upon the piano or organ, or with the voice, only by long and patient *practice.* These arts could never be acquired by reading books or hearing lectures. Mere knowledge will avail nothing in the education of the body.

And the same law applies to *mental* and *moral* as well as physical culture. The child acquires the power to think by *thinking*, and the power of expressing his thoughts by *reciting.* Every mental faculty is developed, and all practical ability is gained, by these two processes. If the mind is educated, study and recitation must be continued through many long years.

The *mushroom* comes to maturity in a *single day;* but the stately tree, whose deep roots, solid trunk, and vigorous limbs, brave the storm and the tempest, is the growth of a *century*. We want no mushroom growths in our families or schools, or in society; and hence I cannot tolerate that false and ruinous system which claims that *knowledge*, and not *discipline*, is the end of teaching. I cannot advise parents to patronize such schools as claim the ability to educate their children by a new process in a few short months. All analogy, all reason, and all experience, point us to the slow growth of Nature's choicest plants as illustrating the true theory of mental development and the true system of education.

It matters little under what circumstances, but in some way the mind must be tasked and trained by patient toil and self-denial for many years to be educated.

Nor is knowledge the end of *moral* culture. The *practice* of virtue alone moulds and matures the good man's character. A knowledge of the divine law is essential as a guide to duty; but *active obedience* alone can form the habit of well-doing, and elevate the man to the condition of the saint.

The popular prejudice against this view of education is based upon the error, that no branches of study are practical which are not brought into immediate use. That this is an error will appear to all who carefully examine the subject. For instance, it is not claimed that the gymnast will need his dumb-bells, rings, and wands, in the duties of active life;

but he will need and use the strength and vigor which these athletic exercises impart at all times and everywhere. The student of books may never find in his business or profession any direct use for the higher mathematics and languages which were required of him in his course of studies; but he will find constant use for the well-trained mental powers and faculties which the study of these subjects has cultivated.

The study of history and literature may not materially aid the laborer in his struggles to gain a living for himself and family; but a knowledge of these branches will impart that intelligence and culture which will elevate the man, and prepare the citizen better to perform his important duties. Every department of study is *practical*, so far as it can cultivate the power of thought and expression, and elevate the human being to a higher grade of civilization.

Still further: every subject of thought and study has some practical bearing upon every other subject. Hence, the more accurate the investigation and the more extensive the knowledge upon collateral topics, the better fitted is any man for the practical use of what he must know to succeed in any given department. Common arithmetic is intimately connected with the higher branches of mathematics; the sciences have no well-defined lines of separation; and the languages, both living and dead, have one common bond of union.

A practical education, therefore, implies not only extensive culture, but extensive and varied knowledge; and the more extensive and thorough, the more practical it will be.

There are in the world two classes of men, — *thinkers* and *doers.* The thinkers are educated: the mere doers are uneducated. The one class are men of *thought;* the other, men of limited *knowledge.* But the educated are far superior to the uneducated. Thinkers are the masters in every department of life, and have been in every age. Patient thinkers have made all the discoveries, wrought out the inventions, and created the science, of the world. Indeed, we owe to these men all the practical advantages that crown our highest civilization.

The doers are entirely dependent upon the thinkers for the knowledge they have of their trade or profession. The undisciplined yeomanry cultivate the soil; but men of culture have created and brought within their reach the science and literature of agriculture. Common sailors can navigate the ship; but the science of navigation and the invention of the mariner's compass are the work of accurate thinkers, who have trained their minds by earnest study to habits of thought and investigation.

The common impression is, that men who have devoted themselves exclusively to abstract study are not practical men. As mathematicians or chemists or philosophers, they seem not to have done much for the world; but, without their *thinking*, there could have been no *doing*.

Bridget makes our bread; but who discovered and taught her to apply the chemical principles by which good bread can be made?

The unlettered engineer may run the steam-car with marvellous skill and success: but who invented the engine? and who discovered the laws of steam, and the application of this motive power to machinery?

The common laborer may manufacture and set up the telegraph, and stretch the wires over hill and dale; limited knowledge enables the mere youth to work the keys, and communicate thought with the rapidity of lightning from town to town and city to city, and even through ocean's dark caverns to distant continents: but who first discovered the chemical laws by which this wonderful art is made possible? and who chained the lightning of heaven, to become the fleet messenger and obedient servant of man? Profound *thinkers* have done all these wonderful things. *Doers* have only employed the knowledge and power which thinkers have placed within their reach.

Who, then, are the *practical* men in practical life, if not such men as Watt, Franklin, Fulton, Stephenson, Newton, and Morse? Yet many doers in every community affect to despise such thinkers, and to regard them as of little consequence in the world. But, as a matter of fact, without the results of the study and toil of such men, common men could do nothing.

Thinkers, after all, *are* recognized, and in a measure appreciated, even by their critics. They do them homage: they go to them for light in the hour of darkness, for guidance in prosperity, and for protection in danger. From the very nature of the case, the thinkers are to the doers as masters to servants; and must forever remain so, unless all shall become educated.

If, then, it is the province of education to impart the power of thinking, it must follow that all who have not acquired that power are not educated. And just here comes in the practical suggestion, that parents should establish such a system of instruction, and adopt such a course of elementary training, in the family and in the school, as will transform all their children into thinkers.

This would, in one generation, destroy the oligarchy which exercises the mastership over the masses in every community; not by crushing out the thinkers who have elevated society to its present condition of civilization, but by educating and elevating *all* to the condition of the few. If knowledge is power only to those who are able to employ it, we shall increase that power tenfold or a hundredfold by adding to it the ability to think.

Education, as here defined, is not for the rich, nor for the poor; not for the mechanics, nor for the farmers; not for the clergy, nor for the laymen: *it is for all.* All our children should acquire the art of thinking. Other attainments and accomplishments without this are of comparatively little importance. But a well-arranged and thorough *disciplinary* course of study will necessarily impart the desired intelligence and refinement.

The prevailing error in regard to the nature of education has led many parents to believe that its only object is to fit their children directly for some trade, art, office, or profession. But thorough mental discipline is alike important for all, and should be secured without special reference to their future employment or profession. When thus educated, they will be fitted for professional instruction under masters in merchandise, farming, engineering, law, medicine, divinity, eloquence, poetry, or painting, as the case may be.

And here we meet another popular error; viz., that our children may be moulded by education into fitness for any sphere of active life as clay in the hands of the potter is moulded into any form. With this false view, the impression has prevailed that all the young men who can pursue a liberal course of study (and many who have only limited culture) *must* enter one of the learned professions. The deluded father is anxious that all his sons should follow in his footsteps, and desires that each should become what he is, — a mechanic, farmer, lawyer, doctor, or clergyman, as the case may be.

And is not this the reason why we have so many unskilful mechanics, indifferent farmers, and *floating* professional men, who have failed to sustain themselves in the positions they have undertaken to occupy? All men and women are fitted by their Creator for some sphere of usefulness. There is some position in which every one could achieve success, and secure honor to himself and profit to others, if he could only find it. How, then, shall our children find their places in the world? This is the practical and important question to be answered.

First of all, parents should see to it

that their children are thoroughly educated. Every one needs discipline, whatever sphere in life he is to occupy. Then he should be left free to consult his own tastes, preferences, and peculiarities; and should be advised only in view of his manifest fitness for the position he is likely to select.

No parent can know whether his son is adapted to the farm, the work-shop, the pulpit, the forum, the sick-room, or the school-room, as well as the son knows himself. Many a failure in life has resulted from parental advice and dictation, or forced professional training. Let all learn wisdom from such failures; and, while they aim to give their children every possible opportunity for culture and improvement, let their own taste and better judgment mark out their future life-work.

How much more honorable and profitable would be these very mechanical arts which clothe and feed us, if all doers were also independent thinkers, and each especially adapted to act the part assigned him!

Do we realize how soon the generation of children who are now being trained in our families and schools will be called into active life? These children will come up to act the part of citizens, parents, officers, counsellors, trustees, school-committees, examiners, and perhaps lawyers, commanders of armies and navies. They will act in a thousand ways where the interests, character, and lives of men will depend solely upon their power of thought, and their adaptation to the places they occupy in society.

Who can estimate the loss of time, the perversion of talent, and the waste of material, from the want of ability to think and act with wisdom and promptness?

How many estates have been ruined and characters blasted, how much good influence has been paralyzed, how many lives lost, and how many governments overthrown, simply from the lack of mental culture, and from the misdirection of mental power!

The end of teaching is to fit our children to achieve the highest success in life. No parent can be indifferent to this result; and hence the wisest means should be employed, and the greatest care taken, to secure it.

A thorough practical education implies the cultivation of the habit of fixed attention. This is not only a condition of success, but the result of successful mental discipline. The habit of perseverance in the midst of trials and disappointments, and of patience to endure the hardships of life, are acquired also in this rigid school of discipline. The taste, imagination, memory, and judgment are cultivated in the very process of disciplinary training; and the conscience, developed under the influence of divine truth, is made the ruling power of the mind and heart. With *such* an education, our children would be thoroughly furnished for their life-work: without it, we can leave them no inheritance that will secure their future success and usefulness.

One more thought in this connection, and I close these chapters upon the training of the family.

The children whom the parents of this generation have intrusted to their care and instruction stand at the opening of the most eventful day, and in the midst of the most stirring scenes, in the history of our world. Let the scenes of the past and the hopeful prophecies of the future encourage us to prepare them, by solid mental and moral culture, for the duties and responsibilities of opening manhood and womanhood. With a mind thus trained to the defence and imbued with the love of truth, they will go forth to guide the storm, and gather up its mingled elements, for the redemption of man and the glory of God.

INDEX.

www.ingramcontent.com/pod-product-compliance
Lightning Source LLC
LaVergne TN
LVHW010217110826
845151LV00004B/1111

* 9 7 8 1 4 2 5 5 2 7 0 5 1 *